MW00761788

THE AFRICAN MEETS
THE BLACK AMERICAN

Kwame A. Insaidoo & Roxanna Pearson Insaidoo

Bloomington, IN Milton Keynes, UK

authorHOUSE®

AuthorHouse™
1663 Liberty Drive, Suite 200
Bloomington, IN 47403
www.authorhouse.com
Phone: 1-800-839-8640

AuthorHouse™ UK Ltd.
500 Avebury Boulevard
Central Milton Keynes, MK9 2BE
www.authorhouse.co.uk
Phone: 08001974150

© 2006 Kwame A. Insaidoo & Roxanna Pearson Insaidoo. All rights reserved.

No part of this book may be reproduced, stored in a retrieval system, or transmitted by any means without the written permission of the author.

First published by AuthorHouse 9/25/2006

ISBN: 1-4259-5867-2 (sc)
ISBN: 1-4259-5868-0 (dj)

Library of Congress Control Number: 2006908215

Printed in the United States of America
Bloomington, Indiana

This book is printed on acid-free paper.

Dedication to the memory of:

Roxanna Pearson's brother, Derrick Pearson, one of the founders of Black Students Union at Buffalo State Teachers College

Ms. Pearson's beloved father, Mr. Roy Pearson of Tuscaloosa, Alabama; her best friend and mother, Mrs. Christine Pearson; and her grandmother, Mrs. Millie Dockery of Greensboro, North Carolina.

Also dedicated to the fondest memory of Kwame's beloved sister, Comfort Akua Serwaa and Kwabena Emmanuel of Akwasiho in Ghana.

And to Kwame's grandparents, Nana Akosua Asieduaa and Afua Nimo Owusuaah of Koodum, and to his late uncle the Right Reverend Afadzi of Saltpond in Ghana.

Our sincere and heartfelt thanks to the late Leo Billy Rolle, founder of United Block Association, Inc. in New York City.

Other books by Kwame A. Insaidoo

- Can the Black Man Rule Himself?
- Is the Bible a Woman's Enemy?
- Anansi And Other African Trickster Tales
  [With Dr. Donald R. Holliday]

Please come closer... I am your brother, Joseph, whom you sold into Egypt.

Now do not be upset or blame yourselves because you sold me here. It was really God who sent me ahead to save people's lives.

God sent me ahead of you to rescue you in this amazing way, and to make sure that you and your descendants survive.

So it was not really you who sent me here, but God.

Genesis 45:4-8

CONTENTS

ONE 1

TWO 13

THREE 53

FOUR 73

FIVE 83

SIX 119

SEVEN 129

EIGHT 167

CONCLUSION 199

NOTES 207

SPECIAL THANKS 211

ABOUT THE AUTHORS 213

ONE

THE AFRICAN HAS BEEN SEPARATED from his black American brothers and sisters since the dawn of the trans-Atlantic slave trade. Millions of black Africans were forcibly ejected from their native soil, separated from their loved ones—their mothers, fathers, sisters, brothers—and torn from the lives they knew and from their various languages they spoke and carried to a strange, cold, and unfriendly land.

Those who survived the brutal Middle Passage and landed in America were further subjected to dehumanizing, abusive, and barbaric torture, and were treated as pieces of property to make their masters' prosperous. Their native African cultures, traditions, languages, and other ways of life were bleached out of them. Their African names were forcibly removed and replaced by their slave masters' names. Their African culture, dignity, personality, pride, self-respect, and resiliency were fiercely challenged by the incessant, dehumanizing lashes, rapes, and violent lynchings frequently used by the slave masters.

Essentially, the black American has become a new person in a new world with a unique experience. After hundreds of years in the new world, coupled with their unique experience, how do they view or see, or relate or perceive, or better yet interact with their African kith and kin they left on the African continent, who are now "voluntarily" joining them in America in exodus proportions, fleeing the life of grinding poverty, deprivation, hunger, dictatorship, helplessness, and all kinds of diseases?

It must be remembered here that the black Africans were not also left untouched to freely develop naturally on their own. The Europeans, in their greedy scramble to pillage Africa's lands and wealth, partitioned Africa among themselves. This greedy scrambling for African lands, mineral wealth, and forest resources further divided and disunited black Africans on the continent against each other. Some Africans were made to believe that they were Frenchmen, some were literally transformed into colonial English subjects, others became black Belgians, yet some became Spaniards or Portuguese Africans. The cultural outlook of the black African changed to reflect that of their colonial masters; hence, an educated African from a French colony in Africa behaved like a Frenchman from Paris and felt more at home in Paris than in his native Africa. Similarly, Africans from British colonies were brainwashed to take the characteristics of their British masters.

To determine how the black Americans perceive or feel or interact or react or deal with the black Africans, the authors—an African from Ghana in West Africa and an African American from Buffalo in New York state—embarked upon an extensive quest spanning over a twenty-five year period, interviewing and speaking to Africans in

America and African Americans from Missouri, Texas, North and South Carolina, New York, California, and other places in the United States.

We began our long. Difficult, and perilous journey of attempting to unravel black Americans' perceptions and experiences in interacting with the exodus of the incoming black Africans, and the response of the Africans to their dealings and relationships with the their black American kith and kin, beginning with the experience of our co-author Kwame A. Insaidoo. We will refer to him throughout the book by his first name, Kwame. *Kwame* in the Akan language in Ghana means a male born on Saturday.

Kwame was born in Ghana, West Africa and before coming to America in 1976; he had heard and learned a lot about the African Americans. Kwame was told by his father, who had not been to America then, that there were Africans sold into slavery who now lived in America. He was told that they looked black, like himself, but could not speak or understand his native Akan language, and they were called Negroes. His father told him that among the Negroes were great and powerful boxers like Sonny Liston, Joe Louis, Mohammad Ali, Joe Frazier, and celebrated musicians like Ray Charles, Chubby Checker, Stevie Wonder, Louis Armstrong, and many others.

Kwame's stepmother, Stella, told him that she knew some Ghanaian students who attended universities in America and brought home some of their Negro wives. She explained to him that those Negro wives controlled and restricted their Ghanaian husbands and did not allow them to go anywhere without their permission. The Negro wives severely restricted the movements of their Ghanaian husbands. The men could not visit any of their relatives, friends, and extended family members without their wives going along with them. She said her friends found the Negro women's restriction of

3

their husbands strange and intolerable, because the Ghanaian male is not used to such restrictive women. Moreover, in Ghanaian society women are not supposed to follow their husbands everywhere they go. Indeed it appeared strange to the average Ghanaian to see wives parading beside their husbands everywhere the husband went. The men need room to socialize on occasion and be with other male friends independent of their wives. She said most of the Negro wives had numerous fierce verbal quarrels with their Ghanaian husbands and eventually got fed up with their husbands and left Ghana to their home country of America. She advised young Kwame that it was not a wise idea to marry those Negro women, because of the huge differences in cultural orientations and variations in societal perceptions of acceptable traditional marriage norms.

At his secondary school, Kwame learned a lot more about the black Americans from his history teachers, who had not traveled to America at any time in their lives. These teachers, who were merely regurgitating what they had read from books, taught Kwame and the rest of his classmates what they knew and had read about the black Americans, which included:

- They referred to the black Americans as Afro-Americans.
- The Afro-Americans were originally Africans who were unfortunately sold into slavery, but they were technically not slaves but Africans whose condition was that of slavery.
- Slave raiders—especially Babatu and Samori—invaded, pillaged, and captured many black African children, women, teenagers, and strong, hardworking males and sold them to the slave traders.

- In Ghana many of the slaves were captured in the northern territories and were marched all the way through the grasslands and forest regions to the coastal areas.
- The barbaric pillaging of African villages was particularly concentrated in the northern territories, where the Arabs had violently destabilized the black Africans, occupied their lands, and violently imposed their religions by subduing the natives with the so-called holy war, Jihad. The Arab slave traders violently captured millions of black Africans and succeeded in selling them off to the Europeans in the coastal regions of Ghana.
- In the coastal regions the white man imprisoned or hid the slaves in large forts or castles that dot the Ghanaian coastline (for example, Cape Coast and Elmina Castles) until the large slave ships arrived to carry them like packs of cattle to the new world.
- In the coastal areas the Portuguese and Spaniard slave dealers usually carried large barrels of whiskey, rum, and other cheap hard liquor to the natives and organized what amounted to large all-evening parties where many unsuspecting natives were made intoxicated, after which they were chained and carried aboard the large slave ships that traveled onward to the new world. For many of them, after the effects of the alcohol wore off, they found themselves in chains, in the packed ship on the way to the new world.
- Some of the African chiefs were bribed with mirrors, beads, muskets, and alcohol to sell some of their captured indentured subjects to the slave traders.

- When the Africans arrived in the new world, they were subjected to all forms of horrible abuses and made to work for many, many hours each day to make their masters prosperous and wealthy. In their misery, the Africans sang songs to lift their spirits up.
- Some of the girls in the class shed tears when they heard the atrocities, barbarities, and inhuman treatments meted to the Africans in the new world.
- Some of the teachers taught that the West African countries where the slaves were taken from are more developed materially and economically than other parts of Africa. They argued that the slave trade had unseen beneficial effects to West Africa. But today such line of reasoning is not only simplistic but dumb and backward, because those teachers should have been trained to think intelligently that it was not the slave trade that made those West African states flourish. But in spite of this odious and barbaric trade, the resilient Africans were able to rise up again.

Kwame related that the first time he saw Afro-Americans was his first year at the University of Ghana. He said they looked very beautiful and most were not like the typical darkened African; most of them were fair in complexion with large afros, leading him to believe that their name *Afro-American* derived from their large, bushy afros.

Kwame's experience with the Afro-Americans before coming to America is not an isolated story. We talked to many Africans from different countries and asked them about their experience or what they knew or thought of the black Americans in Africa before they came to America.

Our friend Omari from Ghana said when he was home in Ghana he believed that the black Americans were their long lost brothers and sisters of the African people. He sincerely and genuinely believed that they also loved and respected their African brothers and sisters back on the African continent. Omari and his friends in Cape Coast were led to believe that when black Americans met Africans, they would take them in and help finance their education, buy them cars, and treat them like their long-lost brothers and sisters who were finally coming back together for a happy and healthy reunion. Omari informed us that when his mother saw the movies of the civil rights marches and demonstrations, where vicious police dogs and waterhoses were deliberately let loose on the black people, she and her friends wept and felt saddened by the inhuman and barbaric treatment the white man was visiting upon the black people. His mother and friends wondered why these blacks would not come back home to their African continent if the whites did not want them to be in America.

Omari said when a group of West African students met in London, where they lived for two years; they were delighted and felt honored to see a lot of their black American soldiers. They were thrilled and fascinated to see them and wanted to associate with them— even to say hello to these brave black American brothers and sisters.

Another African brother, Khalid from Kano in Nigeria, said he was proud to learn that in the financially and industrially developed nation that America is, the black American played a major international role. He told us that his Peace Corp teacher in elementary school was a black American lady who showed them series of movies about the civil rights movement in America. He said the entire class was saddened when they saw the police dogs attacking little black boys and girls.

We spoke with an African from the Ivory Coast, who informed us that before coming to America he was in love with the black Americans, because during the Olympics he saw many black Americans dominate the entire track and field events. He said in boxing tournaments he saw the best boxers were blacks, and in baseball and football he saw the blacks dominate the games.

Obi, an Ibo from Nigeria related that his knowledge of black Americans was confined to what he learned at school. He learned that there were some Africans who were sold into slavery and sent to America to work on the plantations to make their masters' prosperous. He said he did not know how they were treated or lived in America and was very eager to learn about how black Americans managed to survive all these years in a land where they were enslaved.

What we discovered time and again was that the average Africans from the French-speaking countries knew very little about the black America before coming to America. Most of those we spoke to inform us that since they come from French countries, they do not learn much about the English countries; but almost all of them instinctively believed that there were some African people sold into slavery who now live in America.

Fanta from Conakry in Guinea told us that before she came to America, she had been told by her great-grandparents that some Africans were kidnapped by Arab slave dealers and shipped to America, and she was eagerly looking forward to meeting those long-lost brothers and sisters.

Hassan from Senegal informed us that he was told by his forefathers that some of his African brothers and sisters were kidnapped by Arab slave raiders and taken to the island, and then to the white man's country. He said he longed to meet them, see how they looked, and congratulate them for surviving for so many years in the land where their forebears were enslaved.

Idrissa, a Senegalese taxi driver in New York City, said that even though he knew very little about English countries, he had been told that some African relatives were forcibly taken to America to work as slaves. He said he knew in his heart that they would be proud to meet their brothers and sisters from Africa and would help them develop Africa to be like America, because if the whites were capable of developing America on their own, they would not have braved the mighty Atlantic Ocean to get Africans to help build their country for them. His point was that if the Africans who were sold into slavery had succeeded in building America to be a superpower, they could help build Africa to be a great, powerful continent.

Kwame's schoolmate in Ghana Kwakye, who was a member of the Church of the Lord, related this story before coming to America. He said his uncle was one of the elders of the church, and for many years the pastors that came to minister or fellowship with the Ghanaian congregation from North America were all white pastors. One day his uncle summoned the courage to ask the senior white pastor from America why black American pastors were not sent to minister to the black congregation in Ghana? The white pastor responded that they had been looking for competent black pastors to send to Ghana, a black country, but could not find those who could preach and read the Bible well enough to send to represent such great church. Needless to say, when Kwakye got to America and heard powerful black preachers and the numerous articulate black preachers in America who can preach to summon the heavenly angels and lift the multitudes of women and men into spiritual dance, he felt betrayed by the lies of his church elders.

A middle-aged man from the Volta region of Ghana, Komla told us that when he was in Ghana he knew the miserable plight of the Africans who were sold into slavery. He said he and his family and friends were genuinely interested in helping to resettle some of the blacks interested in coming back home to Africa to resettle to a more homey and happier life in Africa. He deeply believed in his heart that the blacks in America would be extremely happy to reunite with their long-lost African brothers and sisters.

We spoke with four African students at the University of Ghana who have never been to America to determine what they knew about African Americans and how they got their information. Jihad, a third-year student, informed us that some original Africans moved to America due to the slave trade but did not indicate to us how they moved there. He informed us that he knew that there are a lot of prominent and highly educated African Americans who have contributed immensely to the development of America and Africa. He mentioned the singular contributions of Dr. W.E.B Dubois.

His friend Ebo said that black Americans are American citizens born out of slavery, and he knew that they are descendants of black slaves in America. Ebo informed us that he has seen films and read magazines that made him believe that the black Americans are friendly people, especially to their African brothers and sisters on the continent.

Baye, another student, informed us that he has read and watched movies about black Americans, has been fortunate to associate with them in Ghana, and knows in his heart that they are helpful to Africans and that most of them sincerely and eagerly want to know more about the African people.

Ofari, another third-year student in Ghana, informed us that he learned about black Americans in history class and was told that they are products of the trans-Atlantic slave trade but are now citizens of America by birth.

Ben, another African from Nigeria, said, "Those of us young boys from West Africa were generally infatuated with black Americans. We loved them, especially their soul music; and we wanted to be like them." He said he was fortunate to have a black American Peace Corp teacher, who taught him at the Polytechnic Institute he attended. He reminded us that the black Americans who came to West Africa generally displayed a positive attitude and genuine respect for African traditional institutions, and were grateful to be in the motherland.

Generally, therefore, the majority of the Africans, especially those we surveyed, who had never set foot in America, viewed black Americans collectively in the following ways:

- Their long lost brothers and sisters who were removed unwillingly from their native land and taken to a strange, cold, and hostile society.
- Brothers and sisters who should at all costs endeavor to return to their native continent to reunite with their long-lost African kith and kin to reclaim their culture and their ancestral lands.
- People to look up to for some financial help. Some Africans on the continent believe that all black Americans have abundant material prosperity, and can assist many Africans out of their financial misery.
- Some Africans want black American professionals like doctors, nurses, engineers, computer specialists, pharmacists, and other business entrepreneurs to come back to Africa. They believe Africa, with its immense mineral resources, bountiful petroleum reserves, enormous

forests and agricultural potential, and abundant cheap labor supply, provides a virgin soil for the technologically endowed black Americans to come and develop the African continent, much like they helped America to develop.

- Black Americans are talented at baseball, football, and boxing. They believe that the best athletes in America are black Americans, because without them American could not dominate the Olympic Games.

- Africans know and love black American soul musicians like James Brown, Roberta Flack, Steve Wonder, Michael Jackson, Alicia Keyes, Marvin Gaye, Otis Redding, Aretha Franklin, Nathalie Cole, Whitney Houston, and the rest of classic talented black people, whose greatness and achievements are internationally recognized and respected.

TWO

THE AFRICAN EXPERIENCE IN AMERICA with the black American is, to say the least, quite interesting, fascinating, challenging, and at times bittersweet.

When our co-author Kwame A. Insaidoo first arrived in America on July 30 1976, he met many Africans from Nigeria, Ghana, Cameroon, Morocco, Senegal, and Gambia, but young Kwame was keenly interested in finding out more about the black Americans he was so fascinated about when he was in his native Ghana. He had learned about them from African students he met on campus who had been in America for some time.

A Nigerian friend, Awo told him that whenever he met a black American male he should raise his hand and make a fist, which symbolized black power. Another Ghanaian student told him, "All that many of these black youngsters here do is buy big cars, ride around, and look for girls in town." Another Ghanaian student took him to his apartment to spend time with him. When the popular television show *The Jeffersons* came on, he told Kwame to watch it well, so he could understand how the blacks live in America.

In fall of 1976, when Kwame finally matriculated at Southwest Missouri State University, he was surprised to see that the black American students segregated themselves from the African students, and each group hardly recognized let alone spoke to the other. In his naive and boyish inquisitiveness, Kwame began asking the African students he associated with on campus why there was such coldness between the Africans and the black Americans students. He wanted to know why the African students did not associate with the black students like they did with the white students and vice versa. He wanted to know what was preventing the two groups from coming together to participate in various friendly activities on campus. Kwame wanted to know whether the African students had black American students as their friends, and if not, what their reasons were. Were the black Americans reluctant to befriend the Africans, or were the Africans too arrogant to associate with the black Americans? Kwame wanted to know the reasons for such indifference and cold attitudes toward both groups of black students on campus.

A Nigerian associate of Kwame's named Olu, from the Yoruba land, was first to answer him. Olu said, "Hey man, you are asking a lot of difficult questions. When I first arrived here last year, I saw the same conditions between the Africans and black Americans students, and I assumed that was the way things were, and I never questioned anybody. I focused on my studies and my campus employment and did not poke my nose into anybody's business. All of a sudden, here you come, young as you are, asking all sorts of questions that we grownups fear to ask." Olu told Kwame if he was sincere in his efforts to find out what was keeping the Africans and black students separated, he would have to write a book as huge as the Encyclopedia Britannica or Americana.

Dissatisfied with what Olu told him, Kwame asked another African student from Gambia, Mustapha about the cold relationship between the Africans and black Americans on campus. Mustapha told him he went to high school with a lot of the black American students and he found out that they do not like African student, period. Of course, Kwame wanted to know why they didn't like the Africans, asking, "What did the Africans ever do to the black Americans?" Was it a personal hatred or an individual or case-by-case issue of dislike of Africans? Mustapha responded, "Kwame, you are fortunate to have a full international academic scholarship that pays for all your tuition, room, and board, insurance, and even pocket money for your entire undergraduate studies. Why don't you concentrate on your academic work and forget about these black people. The white man is trying to lift you up from your peasant background into middle-class America by offering you this huge advantage. The rest of us have to work and do not know whether we will have the money to continue paying our college fees, but you are set for life, and so stop concerning yourself with these black people who will be the first to chop off your neck if they get you."

Still not satisfied with such a self-serving and simplistic answer, Kwame kept asking his Ghanaian friends on campus more about these black people and how to go about befriending, speaking to, and getting to know them so he could understand how they feel about Africans. His Ghanaian friend Yaw told him that he should not go to the black churches because they make a lot of noise and shout a lot in their churches. Yaw told Kwame, "Your blood is too cold and quiet to tolerate the level of noise the blacks make in their churches. When I went to their church I could not sit down for a long time because of the incessant screaming."

Confused, frustrated, and dissatisfied, Kwame persistently focused on the seeming disparity between the African students and the black American students on campus.

Kwame's dormitory mate from Nigeria, Oye, told him in plain language that "Hey, Kwame get it once in your big round forehead that most of these black Americans do not like Africans, because most of them claim that Africans sold them into the slave trade for them to catch hell in the white man's America. To make matters worse, blacks believe that when the Africans come to America the white man treats them better than he treats the blacks here who helped him build America."

Kwame protested to his friend by saying, "Where did the blacks get this false notion that Africans deliberately sold them into slavery?"

Oye told him, "Of course, the blacks read these false ideas from books written by their slave masters who wanted to whitewash slavery and blame the victims of this odious trade on the defenseless, innocent Africans who have been humiliated and victimized over the centuries by these same Europeans."

Kwame told Oye that blaming Africans for selling their brothers and sisters into slavery is truly the Judeo-Christian false interpretation of the odious slave trade. Kwame answered Oye that he was sure that a lot of black intellectuals have read many books written by Afrocentric writers or have listened to oral African narratives to know the real untold story of the slave trade.

Kwame asserted, "The reality behind the falsity of European disinformation and propaganda about the slave trade is the untold story that mean-spirited Arab traders pillaged, raped, and destroyed African villages in the northern territories—fighting, massacring, and capturing Africans. These captured Africans were put in locks and chains and marched hundreds of miles to the coastal areas to be sold to the Europeans." He further asked his friend whether the black Americans were aware that Europeans fought fierce wars with African kings in their unholy attempts to capture Africans into slavery." Kwame informed Oye to tell any black American who uttered the false notion that Africans sold them into slavery that the slaves were not lined up or sitting passively on the beaches of the west coast of Africa, waiting for the Europeans to purchase them as commodities into slavery in the Americas.

Oye agreed with Kwame that the slave trade was not a simple commodity trading or auction, as we are naively led to believe; but the trade was a constant, fierce, hostile, internecine warfare between Arab slave traders and the Africans who were determined not to be captured into slavery.

Now for the first time Kwame summoned courage to approach and speak to a black American student: Leroy, a six-foot-two basketball player who lived in the same dormitory with him. Kwame approached him in his characteristic polite and modest manner, saying "Leroy, can I please ask you a question that has been nagging at my brain all this time?" Kwame asked him why, in his opinion, the Africans and black American students on campus seemed cold and distant toward each other.

Leroy responded, "You are mighty brave little skinny brother man to be asking such emotional questions to people you hardly know and speak to. I guess you must be one of the new African students they just imported here? I must say that I respect your sincerity and naivety, but you are different from the rest of the African students. The rest of the African students associate solely with the white students, date white girls, go to white parties, and seldom come around us, so we figure these people think they are better than us, and so we do our own thing, and the hell with them. Besides, them Africans talk and act differently from us. In addition, brother man, them Africans moves cool, cool, cool, and so cool to become a refrigerator."

Kwame asked Leroy why he referred to him as *brother man.*

Leroy answered, "Aren't you a brother man from the continent?"

After their initial encounter, Leroy and Kwame met frequently to talk about social issues and attend parties together on campus. From that initial meeting Kwame found out that there was a small element of kinship in this cold and strained relationship between the Africans and black American students because Leroy referred to Kwame as *brother man,* meaning deep in his mental recesses, and notwithstanding the constant pernicious societal propaganda, brainwashing, and conditioning black Americans against Africans, Leroy still instinctively referred to Kwame as a brother man from the continent. This assertion meant that there is still unconscious acknowledgement of brotherhood between black Americans and Africans that needs to be honed and developed for the betterment of both peoples.

From this initial meeting with Leroy, Kwame decided to compile his interviews and encounters with black Americans and pass them on to Africans who have not been privileged to travel to America to read and know a little bit about how the blacks in America feel or think about the African blacks on the continent, and also to record African people's responses to black American perceptions.

A funny incident happened when Kwame went to downtown Springfield and waived the black power solidarity greeting fist to a huge black American elderly gentleman, who responded, "Boy, if you don't stop waving that damn fist in my face, I will break it and shove it into your ass." From that day onward Kwame was advised never to waive the black power fist to greet any blacks he met for fear someone would hurt him.

In his relentless and almost obsessive quest to know more about black Americans seemingly hostile, cold, or lukewarm attitude toward black Africans, Kwame approached a black financial aid officer, Jackson, who was assisting his friend Lenny with financial aid paperwork. Jackson, the financial aid officer in his late thirties, told Kwame he had recently obtained his master's degree in sociology from University of California in Los Angeles and had moved to Missouri with his family because of the job offer at the university Kwame was attending.

When Kwame asked Jackson about the seeming hostility or cold attitude, or uneasiness or unfriendly or lackadaisical attitude between the black African students and black American students on campus, he responded by telling Kwame that this attitude (or the apparent schism or whatever you call it) is pervasive nationwide and not confined to this campus only. "This is a microcosm of what prevails nationwide and not just on college campuses," he said. He said this apparent schism between the Africans and black Americans is on the West and East Coasts, in the South and certainly in the Midwestern states of this nation also. He encouraged Kwame to do a formal work researching the nature of the problem, because a lot of sociologists would like to know about how the Africans who have been separated from the black Americans since slave trade and its abolition relate to each other in this new era of masses of Africans coming to America. He said he wished a lot of black and African scholars would do investigative research into this cantankerous issue, and praised Kwame for his foresight, interest, dedication, leadership, and the concern for the betterment of our black race. And he gave him his full support for his pioneering effort at such a tender age on such an emotionally explosive issue.

Jackson said he believed that the black Africans and black Americans represent, from his sociological background and mindset, a sort of "in-group/out-group hostility theory." He said the black Americans represent the "in-groups" in America. These in-group black Americans have their own traditional norms, values, beliefs, cultural mode of doing things, way of dressing, manner of speech, and shared values. He said black Americans have been separated from their African brothers and sisters for hundreds of years and have their own unique cultural experience and style of doing things. He explained that the commonality of their shared, albeit painful, experience has somewhat cemented them together to have this so-called in group behavior. The blacks, therefore, look at the new black Africans coming to America as the "out-group." He said the only thing the blacks have in common with the Africans is their skin color; because apart from the skin color the Africans are like any other foreigners coming to America to compete with them for the scare employment and other resources available to the black Americans. Jackson said the black people are one of the most suspicious people in America because of their unique experience coupled with their shared abuse, torture, and lynchings they have endured in America, and hence are suspicious of the Africans and cannot easily accept them as friends or equals for at least some time—until the Africans prove their loyalty to them.

Kwame asked Mr. Jackson to relate his in-group/out- group theory to the Jews in New York City and their excellent relationship with Jews in Israel and other parts of the world. Kwame challenged him to look at the congenial relationships that exist between the Italian

Americans and those residents in Italy or the Irish Americans and their relationship with those in Ireland.

Kwame reminded Jackson that American Jews support the state of Israel, a Jewish nation, with hundreds millions of dollars each year to insure the survival of their Jewish kith and kin. Kwame further reminded Jackson that the Jews have also been oppressed, abused, tortured, and massacred by Europeans during World War II, and several pogroms endured by the innocent Jews, just like the black people. Yet they are able to band together as a strong, cohesive force for the good of their people. Kwame wanted to know why black people are any different.

Jackson sharply reminded Kwame that the Jews are able to relate easily with each other because of the collective survival of their people and the Jewish religion is the rallying point that serves to cement the diversity of Jewish people in Diasporas and Israel together. He further reminded Kwame that the Irish are singularly united because of their Catholic religion, which binds them to a common religious heritage. Similarly, the Italians' ecclesiastical bond and beliefs in Catholicism creates a commonality of shared beliefs, values, and morals that serve to bind them together. Jackson said, unlike these people, black Americans and Africans do not share the experience of a common religion that rallies them to a greater calling, but instead they belong to a hodgepodge of religiosity and are often antagonistic toward each other.

At the end of the academic year, Kwame was fortunate to meet a soft-spoken well-traveled, decent, and God-fearing black American from St. Louis, Missouri named Wayne. Wayne had traveled to Ghana, Ivory Coast, Cameroon and Nigeria and stayed there for some time and therefore understood some of the mannerisms and behavior of many Africa students a little better. Besides, Wayne was like a big brother to many of the African students in Springfield, Missouri. Wayne, a quintessential Midwestern black American who was a devout churchgoer and participated in many of the activities of his local church, the Bethel Avenue Baptist Church. He also organized civic clubs, church activities, and encouraged African students to mingle with black American organizations in Springfield.

When Kwame met Wayne through a Cameroonian fellow student, they developed mutual admiration and respect for each other. Wayne invited Kwame to attend the all-black-American Bethel Avenue Baptist Church. After attending his first church service with the all-black-American congregation, Kwame related, "The church service was well organized; the choir sang beautiful, melodious, inspiring hymns; and the minister delivered a passionate, moving, and inspiring sermon." Contrary to what his Ghanaian dormitory mate told him, he did not find the church noisy, except for the occasional burst of "alleluya" from the congregation, which was not so different from what he was used to in the Ghanaian churches. Instead of finding the congregation noisy, Kwame reported, "My soul was filled with joy and happiness when I returned to the dormitory. I sincerely thanked Wayne profusely for giving me the opportunity to fellowship with black Americans."

Later that night in his dormitory, Kwame reviewed what the reverend preached to the people in the church. The reverend preached from the gospel according to St. Matthew 25:31-46. It read:

- When the son of man as a king and all the angels with him, he will sit on his royal throne, and the people of all the nations will be gathered before him. Then he will divide them into two groups, just as the Shepard separates the goats.

- He will put the righteous people on his right and the others at his left. Then the King will say to the people on his right, 'Come, you that are blessed by my father! Come and possess the kingdom, which has been prepared forever since the creation of the world.

- I was hungry and you fed me, thirsty and you gave me a drink; I was a stranger and you received me in your homes, naked and you clothed me; I was sick and you took care of me, in prison and you visited me.

- The righteous will then answer, 'when, Lord, did we ever see you hungry and feed you, or thirsty and gave you a drink? When were you ever a stranger and welcome you in our homes, or naked and clothe you?

- When did we ever see you sick or in prison, and visit you?'

- The King will reply, 'I tell you, whenever you did this for one of the least important of these brothers of mine, you did it for me.'

- Then he will say to those on his left, 'Away from me, you that are under God's curse...

- I was hungry but you would not feed me, thirsty would not give me a drink

- I was a stranger but would not welcome me in your home, naked but would not clothe me; I was sick and in prison but you would not take care of me

- Then they will answer him, "when Lord, did we ever see you hungry or thirsty or a stranger or naked or sick or in prison, and we would not help you?

- The King will reply, "I tell you whenever you refused to help one of these least important ones, you refused to help me.

As Kwame listened to the great and powerful words of the reverend, he had a great admiration for the oratorical delivery of his sermon, which sharply contradicted what Kwakye was told by the Church of the Lord's senior pastor. The senior pastor had told him that black Americans could not preach as much as the whites. Here was a black American preacher delivering a sermon like a possessed car salesman moving from aisle to aisle, and singing some of the sermons put the congregation on the edge of their seats with "amen" and "alleluia" flying all over the place. That made Kwame wonder whether the listeners actually practiced what was being preached. Kwame wondered, if the congregants practiced what they were hearing, why were there hostilities toward the African strangers among them who were hungry and could barely pay their rent sometimes? How could the practicing black congregants despise and look down with scorn and condescension on the African stranger among them? Or did they believe in their hearts that these Africans among them would not reciprocate their efforts?

ST. LOUIS EXPERIENCE.

In Kwame's persistent and unwavering determination to meet black Americans all over the nation to find out how they felt about the black Africans and the sort of relationships they had with each other, Wayne arranged for Kwame to travel to St. Louis, Missouri, which is comparably bigger than Springfield. Here Kwame met and spoke with several black people, but the most memorable of all the meetings was the one with a college-educated beautiful lady named Lorraine. Lorraine, as she puffed on her cigarette first, asked Kwame why he was busy going around black neighborhoods in St. Louis, asking about Africans and black Americans. She advised him to stop asking dangerous and emotional questions, because white men would definitely get upset and deport him to his native Africa. She told Kwame that white people do not like to see black men prying into their dirty little secrets of what they have done to separate the black peoples of this world. Nevertheless Lorraine responded by intimating to Kwame, "In the first place, you cannot say 'black Americans,' because America is such a pluralistic society that black people are not simply some monolithic bunch of people here. There are the northern blacks that do not quite get along well with and look condescendingly at the southern blacks, who for their part do not trust the northern city slickers. The light-skinned blacks continue to look down upon their darker-skinned brothers and sisters, and believe they are somewhat privileged more than those whose skin is a darker hue. Moreover, black Americans are mixed with white blood, Indian people, some Chinese people, and a whole lot of other nationalities, and so we are indeed the melting pot of America." Lorraine expressed herself in her proud and dignified manner and spoke condescendingly, beaming with pride and arrogance as if every single African was beneath her. And she asserted with an air of impunity that indicated she believed that Africa is a big jungle filled with wild animals and that she hated Africa because it's full of mosquitoes, malaria, and all kinds of filthy diseases. She said to Kwame, "If Africa is such a good place, why is the huge exodus coming from Africa to America, escaping the horrible famine and other deplorable conditions?" She said arrogantly and proudly that the African does not even get the amount of food to eat that she feeds her dog. And she asked him why she should waste her time to associate with such people.

Kwame did his best to calmly explain to Lorraine that mosquitoes are rampant in the rural areas of Florida, Louisiana, and even Long Island in New York State, but agreed that, indeed, African governments and people must work hard to combat the mosquito problem and prevent the deadly malaria. He told Lorraine that Africa's development had been deliberately and purposively pushed back because of the disastrous effects of both the Arab slave trade and the trans-Atlantic trade. He said it was like a double sabotage against African progress, because it destroyed the moral fabric of African societies. Kwame explained to Lorraine that if hundred million hardworking strong males and females were forced from America today, it would be difficult to develop. Furthermore, If cities and towns were deliberately engineered to fight one another to create perpetual warfare, it will be difficult to have the rapid development you find in America today. Kwame told Lorraine that, in a nutshell, that was what took place in Africa. Kwame further informed Lorraine that the Africans were not left alone to develop their society for their own benefit, because after the slave trade the European powers militarily conquered black Africans again. This time the Europeans exploited and boldly stole the minerals and agricultural products, and forced Africans to become slaves in their own lands for the enrichment of the European nations. "The sad and annoying part of this occupation," Kwame explained to Lorraine, "was that the European craftily convinced our forefathers that the new religion of Christianity expressly forbade them from stealing even an ounce of the gold and diamonds and other agricultural materials from their own land. They said the Africans should carefully guide these items and load them carefully into the European ships to be taken to Europe. The Africans were sternly warned that the Ten Commandments made it abundantly clear that "thou shalt not steal" and any African that stole from the Europeans would definitely go to hell and burn in the perpetual hellfire that is never quenched." They preached as if what they were doing was not contrary to the precepts of the Ten

Commandments, but they had come to steal, pillage, and rape Africa like gangsters.

Kwame further informed Lorraine that it took the modern African freedom fighter like Jomo Kenyatta of Kenya, Kwame Nkrumah of Ghana, Odinga-Odinga of Kenya, Julius Nyerere of Tanzania, Joseph Kaunda of Zambia, Nnamdi Azikwe of Nigeria, Joshua Nkomo of Rhodesia (now Zimbabwe), and a whole host of other African liberators to fight against these entrenched European ideologies and their stranglehold on our people, and to nominally attain independence. These independence movements occurred in the 1960s (barely a decade ago at this time). He reminded Lorraine that Europeans did not go to Africa to develop the place for Africans but went there to create a dysfunctional and backward society riddled with chaos and confusion, which would take time for Africans to untangle to develop their continent. He reminded Lorraine to cast a retrospective glance on the historical developments of Europeans, and even the great United States, and see how many years it has taken them to attain their present level of political and economic maturity. Kwame reminded Lorraine to look at how many wars Europeans waged against each other to finally stabilize their continent, and in her own United States how many wars America waged while settling on the continent; with the native Indians, the Mexicans, and their bitter Civil War, when brothers were killing brothers to prevent the renegade southern states from breaking away. America even endured the assassinations of some of their beloved presidents, like Lincoln and Kennedy.

The meeting ended with Lorraine promising to read more about what the African people had been through historically in Africa, but she repeated her warnings to young Kwame to be careful about such potentially explosive subjects and trying to educate both Africans and black Americans. She said, "The white man would think you are trying to bring about a revolution to topple his civilization." She further advised Kwame to find out what happened to Marcus Garvey from Jamaica, and how he was framed and thrown into jail in Atlanta when the white man felt threatened by the activities of his Universal Negro Improvement Association (UNIA). She continued, "Look, young man, at what happened to our black leaders here in America, before you got here. Malcolm X was feared for teaching blacks self-determination, so they conspired to assassinate him in New York City. Martin Luther King Jr. was a peaceful Baptist minister preaching nonviolence and integration with white people, and preaching about making democracy real to black people. And look at what they did to him. They assassinated him. And before I forget, the Ku Klux Klan has lynched so many young, intelligent black men like yourself who go about trying to help black folks, and so please be careful." Lorraine advised Kwame to concentrate on his college studies and forget about the plight of Africans and the black America, because God eventually intervenes at the proper time to liberate his people from oppression. Kwame thanked Lorraine for her concern and care, and assured her that he was not interested in revolutions but was curious about the coldness, or the great divide or schism, between the black Americans and the Africans.

When Kwame returned to the university campus, he related Lorraine's views on Africa to his Nigerian and Cameroonian friends in the dormitory.

Oye responded by saying, "Kwame, we have told you that these black people do not care much about African people. They really do not like Africans, because most of them believe that we are ignorant, backward, inferior, ugly, and less human than they are."

Oye continued, "Our Nigerian brothers in Washington DC who have lived in America for over twenty years advise us to stay away from these black people, because not only do they dislike us, they are hostile to African people."

Oye told the Africans in his dormitory that the Nigerian brothers told him a sad story that happened to one African student in Washington D.C.

He told the group that one of their Nigerian brothers went to the mean streets of Washington D.C. one night to look for a prostitute. The brother picked up a lady of the night who appeared to be a good-looking lady and took her to one of the motels in the city. When they went to the motel room, the "lady" told him to go to the bathroom and take off all his clothes and come out naked, because he "she" had a wonderful surprise for him. The unsuspecting Nigerian brother obliged. When he came out naked, the "lady" pulled out his gun on him, locked the door tightly, and demanded all his money. He took every dime he had, and then still at gunpoint, ordered him to bend over. The "lady," who was in fact a man in disguise, repeatedly raped him for more than two hours, cursing at him by calling him "jungle motherfucker." And then in a fit of violence and anger, he flung the motel door opened and fled into the dark night. Oye warned all the Africans to be ever so careful about the black Americans, because they could be dangerous to the unsuspecting and naïve African student.

Kwame responded to Oye and the rest of the African students that the Nigerian brother in question should be ashamed of himself for stooping so low as to solicit for a prostitute, instead of staying on campus to meet and nurture mutual friendships with decent God-fearing girls. Kwame continued that the Nigerian brother was really asking for trouble by going into neighborhoods with strangers in a strange country. What happened to the Nigerian brother had nothing to do with the so-called dangerous or wicked black Americans, Kwame further explained. He stressed that the deviant who raped the Nigerian brother did not rape him because he was a Nigerian or an African, but because this brother was in the wrong place at the wrong time and was truly asking for trouble. Kwame concluded that he found it difficult to see how black Americans could be generally categorized as not liking Africans because of the immorality of this misguided Nigerian brother. Kwame further reminded them that this unfortunate incident could happen in any big city in West Africa— like Lagos, Accra, Yaoundé, or Abidjan.

Later when Kwame narrated this story to Wayne, he responded, "If you go out to the trashcan, you will smell the filth."

Wayne and Kwame agreed that the conclusion Oye drew from the barbaric and heinous crime of raping the Nigerian brother was incorrect and faulty thinking simply because the deviant, who happened to be a black American, could have attacked any person: white, Korean, Indian, and Japanese, and any unsuspecting and gullible, innocent black American wondering through the mean streets of Washington D.C. looking for women of easy virtue at the wrong places. They also agreed that there are deviants, criminals, and perverts everywhere in the world—not just black Americans. Wayne reminded Kwame that when he arrived in Africa he was warned to be careful of pickpockets and be careful not to be robbed by the natives. He said that people do not rob you just because you are black Africans or black Americans; they rob anybody they can victimize.

THE OKLAHOMA STUDENT

Later on, Kwame met a black American student, Darrel from Oklahoma City, who told him that he looked at the Africans from far away and wondered why they came here with their kinky hair and very dry skin. But underneath their kinky hair, some of them are really good students, he thought.

Kwame asked him what was wrong with the Africans' kinky hair. He replied that most black Americans think kinky hair makes Africans look really ugly.

Kwame explained to the young man that most African men, particularly in West Africa, like to groom or comb their hair nicely, but many of them seem to think that it is a sheer waste of their time to spend hours upon hours bleaching and using hot combs to process their hair so they can have curly hair like the white man. Kwame said some black American men he has come across spend a lot of their hard-earned money to put Jerry curls in their hair or process their hair to make it look like the white man's. Kwame advised the young black man not look down on or call the African with kinky hair ugly, because the African ideal of beauty is not to look like or blindly imitate his slave master, but to be himself as an African with his God-given natural hair. Kwame reminded the young man that the great civil rights leader, the powerful Rev. Dr. Martin Luther King, Jr. never wasted his time to bleach or process his hair to look like his slave master.

The young black student confessed to Kwame that he never thought that bleaching his hair amounted to rebelling against his God-given black beauty to look like white folks. He said he simply copied or followed what his friends did to look cute to attract the young girls.

A VISIT TO NEW ORLEANS

When Kwame and his Nigerian schoolmate Frank visited their college friends at Tulane University in New Orleans, they met several other African students at campus, and invariably the discussion gravitated toward the sour relationship and the wide schism between African and black American students.

John, a graduate student from Ghana at the university, commented that he genuinely believed the black Americans are Africans' brothers and sisters, and so when he graduated from his undergraduate college in Massachusetts he arranged a big trip with a group of black Americans and a few white students to Upper Volta (now Burkina Faso). He said the black students who went with him were the so-called Afro-centric, dashiki-wearing scholars who loudly mouthed the historical achievements of the black race in antiquity, from Egypt, to Ethiopia, to Timbuktu.

John continued, "When we got to the Burkina Faso, the few white students were busy taking pictures and interacting with the Burkinabe students asking them about the effects of the Sahara deserts on their crops, animal life, and the neighboring population."

John said he was ashamed to see the behavior and the reaction of the Afro-centric black American students. He said they were making fun and laughing at the locals, making fun of how funny they talked, how ugly they looked with their kinky hair, what they ate, and how they were dressed. They ridiculed them as backward and uncivilized Africans. Some of the black American students laughed till they cried when they saw emaciated African women pounding groundnuts and other food in their mortars. John vowed that he would never, ever make any arrangements to take any black Americans to Africa again because of this bad and painful experience he had with them in Africa; however, he would be glad to assist white Americans in visiting and doing research work in any part of Africa.

Then there was this Nigerian student, Sunday, who said that many of his Nigerian friends nationwide refered to black Americans as "akata."

Kwame asked Sunday why Nigerians referred to black Americans as "akata."

Sunday explained to Kwame and the rest of the Africans that an akata is an animal in Nigeria with the following characteristics:

- It is a small animal that can be the friendliest and the nicest to people and can give all its love it has. It can be the best friend anybody can have. It can be extremely playful, show the deepest affection to people, and bring out all kinds of joy to an entire household.

- But at any given time the akata can change to be the people's worst enemy and heap all sorts of insults, violence, and abuses upon people it interacts with. It is hardheaded, and wants to have its own way, no matter what people or friends say or do. It can be downright mean-spirited and display ugly behavior. In sum, the akata is an unpredictable animal, and one cannot know the behavior it will exhibit at any given time.

Sunday said most black Americans he had come across were unpredictable and that most could be the sweetest of human beings you ever met but can change in the twinkling of an eye without any provocation and begin to behave as if they are your worst enemy. He said today they can be your best friends, and the next time you see them they can have an attitude against you, and then on another day you see them all right and wearing smiles on their beautiful faces.

All the Africans burst out laughing, because most had black American schoolmates who behaved in the unpredictable manner that Sunday described. Kwame interjected and explained that the so-called akata characteristics of the black Americans could not be construed entirely in negative terms, considering the inhuman treatment and the abuses they have undergone at the hands of their slave masters.

Kwame explained that black Americans had to be extremely stubborn and unpredictable to survive the ordeal of slavery, the incessant lynching, the frequent raping of the so-called wenches, the unmerciful lashes, the humiliations, and the painful and abusive separations from their loved ones, including their beloved children. Kwame concluded that many black Americans exhibit the so-called behaviors of the akata because they are rightfully suspicious of the motives of anybody they do not know, considering their painful existence in America. Kwame emphasized that African students should read and understand a little bit of the ordeal black Americans have undergone in this country to have a little understanding, compassion, and tolerance and be able to empathize with them and avoid name-calling. Kwame further suggested that Africans on the continent should learn to have some of the attributes of the akata, especially their stubbornness and their unpredictability, because if Africans were as unpredictable and stubborn as the black Americans, the Arab and Europeans slave dealers would have had tremendous difficulty enslaving the Africans, and perhaps the whole slave ordeal would have taken a different turn.

THE MURDER OF A CAMEROONIAN STUDENT

When Kwame and his Nigerian friend Frank returned from New Orleans to their campus, they were saddened to hear that a black American had bludgeoned an African student from Cameroon to death. The African students were beside themselves, and some were understandably fearful or frightened to go around or speak to black American students either on campus or in the small town of

Springfield. Some described the blacks as quick to anger and said they would kill an African with the least amount of provocation. Some of the white students began to exploit the unfortunate incident, telling some African students to be careful of the black Americans. Others would say, "We are your friends and will never hurt you." The African students were so grief stricken and frightened that they hurriedly convened a big meeting on campus to sort things out. Kwame was selected as the moderator of this sad meeting because he had been elected during the previous year as president of the Association of International Students at the university.

During the meeting, a lot of African students vented their anger and some vowed never to speak to the black students on campus again. And some who were understandably fearful of what had happened suggested that all ties be severed with the black American students on campus. Kwame cautioned them to avoid being irrational. He said that, as bitter and painful as the passing of one of their friends and fellow Africans was, they should put the crime in its proper perspective and think carefully about what led to the student's untimely death.

Kwame said, "No one here in this room knew exactly how he was killed and what really happened. The stories we all know are really inconclusive, but one thing we all know for certain is that none of the black American students here in town or on campus have lifted a finger to hurt one of our African students. Our relationship with them is cold, but not hostile. The killers of our friend were criminals from out of town, from faraway New York City."

Kwame reminded the students that the police report indicated the killers were after his car and money, and indeed they stole his car and wallet after they murdered him. Kwame further reminded them that their dead friend was an African who was extending the characteristic African generosity, kindness, politeness, and friendship to people he naively thought would reciprocate. He told his fellow Africans that their friend died because he was still operating under the mindset of the open, honest, decent African cultural milieu he was brought up in and could not conceive of the fact that these people he was extending himself to would turn out to be his killers. Kwame cautioned the African students not to be hostile toward innocent black American students who are also hurt by the passing of a brother man from the continent, as many of the black Americans had expressed their condolences to some of the African students. Instead, he said, they should use the occasion to gradually attend black American functions, parties, gatherings, and churches and to get to know black Americans a little better and begin to have serious social, educational, and cultural interactions with those who are eager to do so.

An Ivorian student, Pierre, agreed with Kwame that these killers did not kill the student because he was an African; they killed him because they wanted his car, his money, and whatever they could lay their hands on. Pierre told them that the killers would have victimized anybody, regardless of whether he was an African or black American or white or Indian or Japanese or Korean or Jamaican. James, a Cameroonian student, also agreed with Pierre and Kwame that these killers did not travel all the way from New York City looking to rob and kill an African student, but they saw an opportunity and the means to execute their diabolical plans upon a victim who happened to be a dear friend.

A TRIP TO CALIFORNIA

When Kwame graduated from Southwest Missouri State University, he moved to stay and work in Anaheim, Orange County in California for six months. While in Southern California, Kwame and his

Ghanaian friends, especially Kweku and Kofi, talked to many black Americans about the sour relationship between Africans and black Americans. Kwame met Jane, a resident of Los Angeles, one Sunday afternoon after church, and they had a lively and animated discussion about blacks and Africans. Jane told Kwame that her main problem with Africans was that they were so mean-spirited that they sold their own African people into slavery in America, where they went through all the abuses visited upon them.

Kwame answered Jane by saying, "Both of us were not around when the slave trade was taking place, so how did you know for sure whether the Africans sold the blacks into the slave trade?"

Jane retorted that she had read in books and seen many documentaries on television that showed how the mean-spirited, greedy, and power-hungry African chiefs were busy trading their own people for muskets, mirrors, beads, whiskey, rum, and other items.

Kwame repeated what he had told black Americans he had met who kept repeatedly asking him the same question. He said the writers who blame the slave trade solely on the Africans are mainly the Eurocentric scholars whose Judeo-Christian interpretation of the slave trade attempted to whitewash and exonerate the European slave traders from their diabolical act and the evils of the slave trade. Then they could cleverly and shrewdly place the blame of the odious trade on the Africans who were indeed the victims of the slave trade. Kwame further informed Jane that other fanatic and demented Eurocentric writers go to great lengths to claim that the slave trade actually helped to Christianize the barbaric African heathens, save them from the evils of the dark continent, and civilize them in the new world. Kwame re-emphasized that the historical truth of what actually happened during the slave trade would be the assignment of truly dedicated Afro-centric scholars from America, Africa, the West Indies, and Europe. It would be their assignment to embark upon a truth-seeking journey backward in time to the African continent to painstakingly research the actualities of the slave trade.

Kwame reminded Jane of the proverbial African folktale from his little village of Koodum near Akwasiho in Ghana. Kwame told Jane that in his small village of Koodum, his great-grandmother, Akosua Asieduaa, and grandmother, Maame Afua Nimo, used to tell the story of the boasting hunter.

The story goes that the hunter was always bragging that it was easy for him to kill tigers in the bush, and he would show off the head of the tiger he had just killed. The grandmothers would finish off the story by saying that the hunter would always continue to boast and brag about the easiness of killing a tiger; until the tigers begin to tell their side of the story. The tiger's side of the story could be entirely different, because the tigers would be able to show how many hunters had lost their lives trying to kill tigers and how fiercely the tigers defended themselves from the hunters.

In Anaheim, California, where Kwame lived, he met a black American woman named Rita who told him that her problems with Africans were many, because she and many of her girl friends had had long interactions and relationships with many Africans during their college days. Rita said she had a lot of black American girl friends who sincerely believed and loved the Africans they married, only to find out that the Africans were just after their green cards to stay in America. Rita continued to say that as soon as those Africans got their green cards, they simply ran away from their black wives. Rita said some of the black American girls later found out that some of the Africans were already married in their countries and had children.

She said, "A lot of you Africans have broken hearts and deeply hurt many black American women just for your stupid green cards."

Kwame responded by telling Rita that they first had to agree that there are many healthy, loving, sincere, honest, and truly beautifully married African men and black American women in America and Africa today.

Kwame continued by saying that many of the African and black couples' marriages lasted longer than many marriages in America. Kwame also agreed with Rita that there are some bad apples from Africa who simple take advantage of some of unsuspecting black American women to get their green cards.

Kwame cautioned that black girls should not jump unadvisedly into quick marriages with people they barely know, particularly when marrying someone from a different continent on the flimsy excuse that they are in love, because marriage is a serious business that can either enhance or seriously damage a person's whole life. Kwame said black girls should thoroughly check the background of the proposed husband before consenting to any marriage arrangements. He said it is important for black girls to read and research the cultures of the intended husbands to see what they are getting themselves into. Kwame indicated that since marriage is an important step for everyone, particularly women, it is significant for the ladies to insist that the intended husbands take them to their countries to meet their parents. Once a black girl visits the home country of her intended husband, she will be able to find out more about all the lies or truths she has been told, and then she can find out more about the background, the family structure, religious practices, and what type of person her intended husband is. The woman can find out if the intended husband's parents truly agree to the proposed marriage and can sincerely give their blessings to the marriage, because this is an important precondition to the success of many African marriages. And then a black American woman would definitely know the true character and the secrets of her intended husband. Among the secrets that they black women can uncover are:

- What kind of a man the intended husband really is and the nature of his family. Is his father a wife beater, or does the family have a violence streak in it? What kinds of hereditary diseases are endemic in the family (like a family history of diabetes, hypertension, and mental illness)? This kind of information is critical for the well being of the children, who are likely to be born into the proposed marriage.
- Does the intended husband already have a wife and children, or he is already betrothed or engaged to be married to someone in his home town?
- It is needless reiterating to state that, by meeting the intended husband's African parents in his country, the black ladies would know his level of seriousness, deep commitment, and the investment a man is making in the proposed marriage. A black woman would know that a man is not merely playing games, as some men actually do to merely obtain a green card, hurting so many unsuspecting, innocent black American women.

Kwame continued to tell Rita that since marriage is a two-way process, the African men should also find out more about their intended black American wives. The man should also go to visit the fiancé's parents to find out what type of family raised the woman, what the woman did (or her lifestyle in her town or city), and determine the following.:

- Whether she was a lady who had many boyfriends, and the level of her emotional stability in maintaining relationships. Was she a lady who was sleeping around with different men—someone who wants to hide her past and settle down with a foreigner who does not know her past? Was she dating with every Tom, Dick, and Harry—and perhaps Jane—in her youthful days? Is she a reformed alcoholic or a chronic substance abuser, and does she secretly abuse drugs?

- Does she have kids who are being raised secretly by her mother, and has she deliberately refused to inform the man? And above all, do the parents approve of their daughter marrying a man from a different continent?

All this information should be openly discussed before the couple can even entertain the idea of marriage.

Kwame told Rita that marriage is such a serious and important undertaking that both parties should invest a lot of time and make extensive preparations before finally getting married.

Kwame and Rita concluded that marriage as an institution is challenging, but marrying a total stranger from another culture can be daunting and an awesome responsibility, and sometimes a downright frustrating enterprise. Kwame told Rita that he has many African friends in New York City who are married to black American women and have a lot of difficulties and challenges getting along because of the seemingly insurmountable cultural problems and lack of respect in the relationships.

Kwame continued, telling her that many of his African acquaintances living in New York City complained bitterly that many of the black American wives do not like to prepare meals at home for their husbands. Some claim that even though their wives do not work and stay home, they still refuse to cook for the family. Some claim that their wives simply like to eat out at expensive restaurants all the time and some "pig out" on fast foods or other junk foods, leading to both their wives and little children becoming obese, which becomes a health hazard to the family.

Rita responded by saying that many of us were brought up in America (especially those of us from big cities) to have a good time and socialize by eating out at our favorite nice restaurants.

Kwame agreed with Rita that eating at restaurants sometimes is good and healthful, and provides for all varieties of food, but couples should not spend their hard-earned money to eat out all the time. He continued by telling Rita that some of those Africans he knows in New York complain that frequent eating at restaurants is putting them in the poor house. Some remark that they came to America to escape the grinding poverty in their countries, so they want to save and invest their money to acquire properties and not eat it all up in restaurants. Some claim that since food is extremely inexpensive, if couples learn to prepare their own meals at home, they would be able to save a lot of money to move up the economic ladder, but like the Ashanti proverb, "they do not build their house in their stomachs."

Rita retorted that "if these Africans cannot afford the black American girls, they should not marry them, because many of these black girls are starving for affection and want to feel and be loved. And as long as they can afford to pay their monthly bills, they want their men to show them good time. The good times include what many of you African men call 'expensive' and 'a waste of money'—eating at our favorite restaurants, going to movies on weekends, attending clubs and parties, occasional weddings, going to amusement parks, and sometimes going out of town to stay in hotels and enjoy activities in other places. You see, many of these black women have been abused or taken advantaged of for far too long, and many understandably crave or are truly famished for true and sincere affection—love that many of you Africans can't seem to provide."

Kwame agreed with Rita that there is nothing wrong about participating in some of these social activities sometimes, but when it becomes constant and repetitive, then the couples cannot save money for possible investments to move up the social ladder. Kwame said a lot of black women and Africans eagerly want to move up the social ladder, and sometimes it takes some amount of discipline and determination to create a family budget and set aside a small savings every payday for the couples to build an egg nest for the family. If the couples can afford to enjoy all the social outings, still maintain their household budget, save money for their children's college, save a down payment for their first home, and invest in mutual funds or certificate of deposits or money market accounts or even purchase savings bonds, then more power to them. Kwame finished off by saying that these financial assets will help make the marriages more secure and stable, because most arguments in marriages revolve around money.

Rita interjected that she had a friend who complained bitterly to her that she once had a joint account with her Nigerian husband, whom she loved deeply, but the husband took all their money in the savings account and ran away to Nigeria, and she never saw him again.

Kwame answered that if her friend had insisted on going to Nigeria to meet the husband's family before the marriage, it would have been difficult for the husband to contemplate stealing all their savings and running away, because the wife would have been able to trace him back to Nigeria and have him arrested or demand her portion of the money. He also advised that the wives should insist on joint bank accounts that require both signatures for any withdrawal, and if the bank violates this agreement or stipulation, then the bank would be compelled by law to compensate the injured party.

Rita agreed and claimed, "I wish many black girls would follow this advice. It would save a lot of them from unnecessary headaches, and it would be difficult for the African men to take advantage of them."

On another front, Kwame also said that some of the Africans in New York City complained bitterly that when they returned home from work their black American wives would sit in their apartments with their female friends and get high on marijuana and liquor while playing loud music. The Africans involved in such horrible relationships could not accept the continuation of this undisciplined behavior of their wives, so most of them divorced their wives once they received their green cards.

Rita responded that they could have worked through this difficulty by going to marriage counseling, if they truly loved each other, but Kwame said he blamed the Africans or any black man who married these girls, because they knew full well that the women had marijuana and liquor problems to begin with.

Kwame further added that some of the Africans complain that some of the black American ladies they date are not completely honest with them, because most have other boyfriends and still keep the Africans on the side. The African men complain that they are afraid of getting physically hurt by the women's overly jealous black American boyfriends, and there are many instances of Africans getting physically hurt by black American boyfriends of these two-timing black girls.

Rita said, "That is the lesson for the African: not to jump into quick relationships with any good-looking black woman they meet, but to investigate their backgrounds." Rita continued by saying that a lot of black American women complain that the African men like to have multiple girlfriends and cheat on their wives a lot. She complained that black women in this country frown on this promiscuous behavior of the African.

Kwame told Rita that black women should educate their African husbands that such behavior is ungodly and disobedient to God's commandment of 'thou shall not commit adultery,' and also, the women must not secretly date and cheat around with old boyfriends and lie to conceal their affairs.

A BRIEF STAY IN HOUSTON, TEXAS

Kwame eventually left Anaheim, California and moved to Houston, Texas with his Ghanaian schoolmate, Afari, to spend the entire summer there. In Houston, Texas they resided on Eagles Street in a relatively quiet neighborhood.

While in Houston, Kwame met a black lady named Jackie, who told him that she was once married to an African student for over five years and she found him to be arrogant, domineering, and difficult to live with. Jackie said she called him arrogant because, "he acted like his shit didn't stink and had a know-it-all attitude." She said most of the African men she had met and gone out with talked to women in a condescending manner, treating them like children. She said many African men do not necessarily speak to their wives; they instead scream and get overly excited over insignificant things that the average black American male would laugh off. Jackie said, "The African male becomes excessively emotional and easily gets upset over trivial and insignificant things, and begin to scream sometimes."

Jackie further explained that the African becomes excitable and loud when explaining minor things to people. And when he gets excited, he will not listen to anyone but can talk frantically for a long time, and you can see the sweat pouring down his face.

"And above all they talk very fast, and you can hardly understand a word they are saying," Jackie said of Africans.

Kwame agreed that many Africans he knows talk excitedly when they want to emphasize something they deeply believe to be true. Kwame explained that he believed most Africans speak with some degree of emotion because Africans are naturally emotional, warm, and friendly people. Moreover, the various African languages have accents and expressions that lead the speakers to accentuate their words in a way that makes them appear to be excited.

Jackie responded by saying that the manner of expressing themselves in loud, excitable tones offends many of her girl friends who have had some dealings with Africans. Jackie continued, "It offends us because when the vast majority of my friends listen carefully to Africans express themselves like they are angry or annoyed with them, they wonder why they behave like that."

Jackie's brother Kevin explained that he believed Africans act this way because of their intrinsic arrogance and overbearing attitude. He said you can smell and see their arrogance and unreasonable pride in their body language and in how they turn their noses up like they own the world.

Kwame answered Kevin by telling him that Africans are indeed proud people because they love and respect themselves. Kwame said that Africans come from an ancient aristocracy and proud culture, and inherited a beautiful continent endowed with vast natural and agricultural resources. Kwame continued that the condition of black Americans has been for many years that of forced servitude and abuse from the slave master who has forced them to play second-class citizens. Hence, when they see a proud and dignified African who acts in a dignified manner, feels good about himself, and is not afraid to display his sense of worth and pride, blacks tend to equate that with arrogance.

Jackie asked Kwame whether the African pride and ancient aristocracy makes them shake their fingers when they talk. She said many black Americans feel offended and insulted when Africans talk by shaking or pointing their fingers at them, because it reminds them of how the slave masters used to shake their fingers at the slaves, warning of some mean impending punishment.

Kwame explained to Jackie and Kevin that many Africans talk by gesturing with their fingers, hands, heads, and any part of their bodies to demonstrate how they feel and what they are saying. A common gesture is talking while opening their palms to demonstrate their sincerity and honesty in what they are trying to convey.

Jackie agreed that if gesturing was their traditional way of expressing themselves, then it doesn't make sense that Africans like to show off to the black Americans that they are princes and come from royal families with so much land and money? Jackie continued by saying that she resents hearing the brothers from the continent talk and brag about all the money and properties they have back home. She said, "If they had all these properties and assets back home in Africa, then what the hell are they doing here performing all sorts of menial work that the average black American would not do?"

Kwame advised Jackie and Kevin that if they heard something that is too good to be true, it sure is, and he said, "Be sure not to believe everything you hear, because people in general play many games to get what they want." Kevin repeated that he knew a lot of them "pretend to be what they are not, because if they had all these things, simple logic tells me that they would not be trying so hard through any means to get to America; and hustle and struggle to make a living like all of us."

Kevin continued that he had met many good and friendly Africans, but what he detested about them is that when you hold a conversation with them, some of them would sometimes begin to speak in their native tongue to each other. Kevin added, "I find that to be rude, offensive, disrespectful, and uncomfortable because it makes me feel like they are saying something bad about me that they do not want me to hear."

Jackie agreed that "if they speak English, and we all can understand the conversation, isn't it rude and annoying that they jump into their native tongue, knowing full well that we Americans do not understand their language? I find this practice among some Africans to be rude and inconsiderate, and whenever I find myself in such situations, I do not waste my time talking with such selfish people, and sometimes I tell them to speak English so we can all understand what they are saying."

Kwame agreed that it can be annoying when people deliberately speak in their foreign tongue knowing full well that others in the room cannot understand what is being said.

Kwame related his experience of the issue to Kevin, Jackie, and Afari. He was at a dinner party with a group of predominantly Ibo students and one Ghanaian lady, Comfort, and all of a sudden the Ibo students began speaking their Ibo language. Kwame and Comfort, not to be outdone, broke into their Akan language, and all the Ibo students began screaming, "Speak English speak English."

Comfort responded, "You see how it feels, when all of us can understand English. You guys were busy speaking your Ibo language, as if you were gossiping about us. Do you now see and feel that such rude and inconsiderate behavior is uncomfortable to say the least?" The Ibo students promised that they had learned a valuable lesson and that they would desist from the practice. But an African businessman in New York City disagreed and said that if he is already speaking his native tongue with his countryman and an American friend walks in on them, he will continue to speak his native language and ask the American to excuse them. He added that if the same American walks in and hears two Frenchmen or Portuguese speaking their foreign languages, he would love to hear them continue to carry on with their conversation in their beautiful language, but if people are speaking in an African dialect, they will complain bitterly that they should speak English.

Before leaving the conversation to go home, Jackie finally said that even though she was married to an African she had no intentions of ever going to Africa. She said, "I do not want to lose my vagina." Kwame was shocked and shy at the same time to hear what Jackie had said, and he did not know what she meant. But Afari reminded Kwame that Jackie was referring to the ancient barbaric custom of female excision among some African tribes. Jackie said, "Afari, you know I am right because I have seen so many documentaries on television showing how these innocent and unfortunate girls lose their vaginas in Africa."

Kwame said he knew little about this savage practice because among his people, the Akans of Ghana, such barbaric female mutilations and abuse are unheard of.

Afari, however, knew more about what Jackie was talking about. He informed them that the Arabs introduced the practice of female excision to African people during their conquests and subsequent spread of their Moslem religious practices. Afari affirmed that this primitive ritual is prevalent in the predominantly Moslem parts of

Africa. Afari said the Moslems have a tradition of marrying many women and it was their belief that the female clitoris made women unnecessarily promiscuous. And so by excising the clitoris women became less promiscuous and confined sexual intercourse to the husband only. Afari continued to say that many Arabs and their African converts to Moslem believed that the clitoris easily got infected because of the scarcity of running water in the desert areas where they dwelled. Their theory was that if the clitoris were excised it would slow down the rate of clitoral infections and insure sanitary conditions among the female populations.

Kwame said this primitive practice amounted to female mutilations and abuses, and that governments in those areas that continued the practices into this modern era must move heaven and earth to stamp out such heinous and abusive mutilation of innocent women.

While in Houston, Texas Kwame and his Ghanaian schoolmate, Afari, attended an all-black-American church. The officiating Reverend James preached brilliantly with an impeccable command of the English language. His sermon was so moving that some members of the congregation were praising the Lord all the way to the bitter end. The Rev. James preached that black people have suffered many iniquities in America and have rightfully become suspicious of foreigners and people from different communities. He intimated that blacks should not waste their time and resources to help the incoming exodus of the black Africans escaping poverty and diseases, because "maybe God is trying to punish them for the sins of their forefathers selling their kith and kin into the slave trade." The Rev. James preached, "You do not know who they are, whose they are, and what their motivations and missions are; and helping them will incur God's wrath for assisting people God is punishing or teaching them a lesson for the sins of their forefathers."

Afari listened with anger in his face and commented to Kwame that such hypocrites and ignorant preachers should be banned from preaching hate from the pulpit. Afari continued to say in anger, "Such preachers should be banned from misleading their congregation, because if God intended to punish wrong doing in slavery, then the slave master, who abused, raped, and lynched God's children should be the one to receive God's severest punishment. But look at them today; they are the ones with the great scientific and technological advancement, with abundant material prosperity unparalleled in the annals of history." Kwame added that the Rev. James is a total disgrace to his race because he is lying to his people instead of educating them about the true conditions of black people in the global economy. Kwame concluded that if Rev. James was an upright man, he could have informed his congregation about the rape of Africa during slavery that destroyed the social, economic, and political stability of black people in Africa. The Rev. James could have further informed his people that after slavery Africans were once again targeted by Europeans for another round of slavery, code-named colonialism, to further enrich the slave master for many years. Kwame concluded that this form of colonialism and naked exploitation further impoverished the African people. Kwame added that if the Africans were running out of poverty and hunger, the slave master helped create these conditions on the African continent.

Kwame and Afari decided that if the xenophobic ranting they heard in the church was the dominant thought pattern of southern black American religious elites, they better leave Houston, Texas hurriedly and head for the more developed and enlightened parts of America, preferably the East Coast cities like New York.

THREE

KWAME AND AFARI RETURNED TO Springfield, Missouri once more to say farewell to their friends, college students, and some residents of the city.

Kwame immediately looked for his old pal, Wayne, who generously accommodated him for more than a month, during which Kwame attended several church services and political forums with him. Prior to Kwame's departure to New York City, in the summer of 1980 he accompanied Wayne to a voter registration taskforce committee meeting at the Bethel Baptist Church annex building. During the meeting Kwame was introduced to the executive secretary of the taskforce committee, Ms. Roxanna Pearson, who was also a nurse. After the meeting, Kwame informed Ms. Pearson about the research he had been trying to do since 1976 concerning the sour or cold relationships between Africans and black Americans. Ms. Pearson responded that, she came from Buffalo in upstate New York and had been involved in similar work since the days her brothers were going to college.

Ms. Pearson informed Kwame that she had been involved in black and African student activities through her older brother, Derrick Pearson, who was the first student to organize the Black Students Union at Buffalo State Teacher's College. She said her brother, who was Afro-centric, was instrumental in organizing some of the black students to make their first trip to Uganda in East Africa. Ms. Pearson said, "Through Derrick, I met and interacted with a variety of black and African students at the college and got to know about the sour and often bitter relationships between the African and the black students."

Ms. Pearson said she had another older brother, Terrance Pearson, who was deeply in love with an African girl, Amma from Ghana. She said Terrance even proposed to marry her, but to her utter dismay Amma's parents did not want to have anything to do with her brother Terrance, and whenever Terrance went to visit Amma they ignored him by speaking their native language, making him feel uncomfortable and unwelcome in their house. Amma's parents informed my brother that she was already betrothed to another Ghanaian and was merely awaiting the customarily rites before the actual marriage ceremony. Ms. Pearson told Kwame that his brother Terrance felt rejected, he said. "I began to dislike those Africans because I believed that they thought they were better than my family. I arrived at that conclusion because that African family lived in an exclusively white neighborhood and behaved like some bourgeoisie family with no black American friends that I knew of."

Kwame explained to Ms. Pearson that many Africans take marriage seriously. Kwame said that perhaps Amma's family concluded that Ms. Pearson's brother Terrance was not ready to marry their daughter because he was barely twenty years old and a college student who was living at home with no employment. And he had no meaningful income base to support himself, let alone a wife and the possibility of a new baby. Kwame asked Ms. Pearson what would have happened if her brother had married Amma and right after the marriage they had a new infant. How was the baby going to be cared for? Who would take the responsibility of caring for the new infant, considering the fact that the brother was still an unemployed student? Kwame told Ms. Pearson that the fact that her brother Terrance and Amma were young, immature, unemployed, and dependent financially and emotionally on their parents meant that they were not financially stable enough to consider marriage. In the light of the circumstances, it is inappropriate and rather unfortunate for Ms. Pearson to jump to the premature conclusion that Amma's parents disliked black Americans, because all they were doing as loving and concerned parents was protecting both youngsters from committing marital suicide.

Ms. Pearson and Kwame met on many different occasions to prepare and plan the outline, scope, and methodology of the work to be done. After more than six months of their initial work, Kwame left for New York City, while Ms. Pearson sought a transfer back to her hometown of Buffalo in upstate New York to work at the Veterans Hospital and be with her aging parents.

THE HARLEM EXPERIENCE

When Kwame arrived in New York City he settled in Harlem, USA, as the locals affectionately refer to the place. Kwame stayed in Harlem with his black American friend Donald, who had moved from North Carolina to Harlem twenty years ago. Donald and family welcomed Kwame with open arms and gave him accommodations free of charge for more than six months, until Kwame eventually secured employment. Donald's son Fred helped Kwame navigate the complicated New York City subway system, teaching him the names of the various trains and their various destinations. To Kwame, Fred would always be an angel who helped him settle in New York City. As Fred took Kwame around the city, he explained that New York City is highly segregated into black Harlem, Spanish Harlem, Washington Heights filled with immigrants from Santo Domingo, El Barrio of Puerto Ricanians, Little Italy, German Town, Little Odessa for Russians, Chinatown, Greek Town, Orthodox Jewish neighborhoods, Howard Beach, West Indian neighborhoods in Brooklyn and in Jamaica, Queens, the Village (where same-sex relationships are common), the famous Benson Hurst, and many other segregated neighborhoods. He advised Kwame to be careful as he moved about in different neighborhoods, because some are less tolerant of black people. Donald, Kwame's graceful host, was called Brother Donald, because he belonged to the Garveyite brotherhood. Brother Donald introduced Kwame to the Garveyites, who are the remnants of Marcus Garvey's Universal Negro Improvement Association in New York City. Their leader was an old eccentric man named Brother Henry, who for almost one incredible year befriended and lectured Kwame on the research he was undertaking.

Brother Henry had formed his own organization and changed the name of the Garvey movement to, the African Nationalist Construction Movement, whose motto was "one God, one nation, one people." Brother Henry theorized that most black people who went to colleges and universities in America and Europe has been brainwashed by the colonialist incessant propaganda, which is mistaken for education. He emphasized that both the black Africans and the black Americans have been brainwashed by the propaganda of the slave master, who is also the brother of the colonialist. Henry told Kwame that the sour relationship between the Africans and the black Americans is a clever tactic of the slave master to divide the African race on both sides of the Atlantic Ocean for easy exploitation. He said the colonialist has poisoned or put a curse in the in the minds of both blacks and Africans with his incessant negative propaganda, attempting to make them believe they are different people. But the slave master unconditionally accepted and gave full citizenship to his poor white brothers and sisters who reached the shores of America, fleeing poverty in Poland and Eastern European countries. Brother Henry taught Kwame that the black Americans are living in abnormal conditions in the various plantations they call their neighborhoods, Henry said, "It is abnormal because most of our households are headed by our women, while most of our men are incarcerated in the big house while the children are unsupervised and running wild in the streets, committing all kinds of heinous crimes." He said that in the middle of this abnormality the light-skinned brothers and sisters who are the offspring of the slave master look down on the dark-skinned blacks in this nation. Of course, the light-skinned blacks get all the special treatments in schools and workplaces in America. He also referred to them as house Negroes, meaning they were the blacks who stayed around the slave master, whereas the dark-skinned blacks were referred to as field Negroes. They did most of the menial work and other dirty-work nobody cared to do.

Brother Henry told Kwame that the black Africans have the same problems because those who are Western educated tend to look down upon the masses of Africans, thinking of themselves as better because of their Western propaganda education. Henry taught Kwame that the slave master's long-term master plan is to prevent the black Americans and Africans from coming together, because if they do, the slave master knows that would be the downfall of his dominance over the black race and a diminution of his global power. Kwame asked Henry how that could bring about a diminution in the slave master's global power. He answered that the black Americans have lived for hundreds of years in this highly developed scientific and technological society and have acquired these skills. He said there are vast amounts of black American military and industrial experts with advanced technical expertise: computer programmers, electricians, geologists, bridge builders, managerial experts, medical and pharmaceutical personnel, and a whole host of other experts. And then look at the continent of Africa, filled with all kinds of mineral resources, gold, diamonds, bauxite, phosphates, aluminum, petroleum, uranium, and abundant, untapped hidden resources coupled with the huge continent and the masses of strong and industrious black people.

Brother Henry continued that the slave master is wise and shrewd enough to theorize that if the skilled black Americans were to join hands with the black Africans on the continent, they could build a strong and powerful civilization that would be hostile to his interests, considering the hostile treatments they meted to black people on both sides of the Atlantic. "Is it therefore surprising," Henry asked Kwame, "that the slave master would move heaven and earth to separate the Africans from these black Americans?" Brother Henry continued by saying that "if the slave master allowed the black Americans to leave America, could you imagine how boring American would be?

- There would be no powerful black athletes to win many of the Olympics gold medals for America. Africa with its masses of black people, would dominate the Olympics.

- Those baseball, football, and basketball stars would be gone from America, and so during the so-called World Series America would always lose to Africa.
- The soulful music that reverberates and energizes America would be gone to Africa, and America would be a dull place without its soul, entertainers, comedians, etc.
- Billions of dollars that black Americans pump into the American economy would be lost, together with their immensely skilled people.
- Several economic structures in America revolve around black people, and these would be gone forever
- And eventually America would lose its competitive edge to the European Union and China.
- All the powerful and spiritual black preachers and gospel music would be gone to make another continent powerful.

Brother Henry concluded that the slave master is aware of the vital importance of black Americans to their country and would move heaven and earth to keep them in America.

Brother Henry said, "Why do you think that Marcus Garvey was set up, implicated, and eventually imprisoned in Atlanta, Georgia? Because his Universal Negro Improvement Association had become so powerful that millions of black people were ready to follow him to form a new African government; something the slave master would never allow to happen." Henry said the slave master knew that Mr. Garvey was not playing games when he set up the Black Star Line in 1921 and put ships on the high seas, ready to sail to Liberia and the rest of West Africa.

Brother Henry repeated that the crux of Kwame's decade-long obsession of the sour relationship between black Africans and black

Americans is the slave master's deliberate propaganda, intended to divide both people.

Another brother Winston of the nationalist movement said that slave master did not want to see the blacks leave America but wanted all of them dead right here on shores of America. Brother Winston said the slave master read the Bible and knew what happened to Egypt when the slaves (Jews) left. He said Egypt collapsed and so they feared that if the former slaves left America, a similar fate would follow.

Brother Winston said, "It is not true that black Americans do not like Africans, but America is such a diverse nation with many black with different orientations. You know, black people in America are not some monolithic people; there are all different people with different societal outlooks and different ideas." Brother Winston continued that you would find some blacks that do not want to have anything to do with Africans. He continued that in New York City Kwame would come across black people who are more Afro-centric or more African than many Western-educated Africans. He said many black Americans have the same right to African lands as Africans and when the hour comes nobody in Africa can stop them from claiming those lands on the continent.

Brother Winston related a weird story to the nationalists assembled there. He said when the so-called crazy General Idi Amin Dada of Uganda appealed to the slave master for some black Americans to come to help Uganda develop, the slave master sent only Uncle Toms to spy and report what Gen. Amin was up to. He also said many Ghanaians, including the late President Kwame Nkrumah, believed that the black American Ambassador Franklin Williams was instrumental in the 1966 coup. Brother Winston said, "All these alleged black sabotages against African governments have nothing to do with the masses of the black people. African governments must do their own research in America to find clean, Afro-centric black Americans willing to work to develop Africa, and stay away from these Uncle Toms."

He said there are many black Uncle Toms in America who will sell their own people for a bowl of rice, and so when Africans come into contact with black Americans they should be careful to know whom they are dealing with. Brother Winston said the same Uncle Toms are available in Africa also. He concluded that we cannot make a blanket statement that black Americans do not like Africans, but we can sure say that we have enemies within the race both in America and in Africa.

Brother Watusi, another tall six-foot-two black American, said the same forces oppressing and exploiting Africans are also against black Americans. He continued by saying, "Whether we like it or not, we are one and the same people, but we have a knife stuck in our backs to act the way we do. We cannot help but love Africa, because we are fighting for the same cause to liberate our souls and have a decent life on this planet that belongs to all of us, and not just to some selected race of people."

Later as the nationalists got to know him, Kwame was given the opportunity to attend one of their secret meetings. At the meeting Kwame discovered that their mission was the same as that of Marcus Garvey, because they believed that Garvey's ideas are not dead but that there is a continuum from Garvey to Carlos Cook to Brother Henry. Their fundamental idea is essentially back to Africa; and the philosophy of Africa for Africans that Garvey espoused in the 1920s. Their philosophy is to trade with the motherland. They believed that if one hundred people can invest 1,000 dollars, they can accumulate 100,000 dollars to purchase land and begin lucrative businesses with Africa and in time can resettle interested black Americans in

Africa. The group works closely with the southwest African country of Namibia and Ivory Coast in West Africa.

The group claimed that they had actually acquired lands in Ivory Coast, where they wanted to pursue business transactions with the Ivorian people. Brother Watusi commented, "You see, brother Kwame, these black Americans you have met here in New York City consider themselves Africans who are sick and tired of living under intense oppression in America and are ready to move to Africa. And some of us may get there before you even go back home to the continent. You are in New York, not some backward southern state or lily-white prejudiced Midwestern state where the blacks have little knowledge of themselves and of Africa." He continued to say, "You will find out that many of the blacks here are more Afro-centric than you are."

Brother Henry added that many black Americans and some Western-educated Africans have received the propaganda education of the white supremacist, and this systematic propaganda is at the root of all the problems of black Americans and Africans.

Brother Henry taught that this white supremacist propaganda education begins with the deliberate distortion of African history, which teaches the world that black people have never had any civilization, have lived in the dark continent of Africa, and have not made any contribution to modern civilization. And it teaches that it took the white man to civilize them. Henry said the real hidden history of the black race began centuries ago in Egypt and that black people built all the pyramids in Egypt. Henry said Napoleon's soldiers chipped the nose off the Sphinx in Egypt to disguise its black features. He said Greek scholars stole most of the ancient black scholars' writings in Egypt when Alexander the Great invaded Egypt. He repeated that the Egyptian libraries were burned down after the valuable scrolls and treasures were looted from the ancient library of Thebes in Egypt.

Brother Henry said his message to most black scholars is for them to continue to undertake consistent and systematic research to prove that modern civilization owes its very structural foundation to Africa and Africans. He asked, "Why would the slave master brave the mighty Atlantic Ocean to come to African and carry these Africans to build this country for them? Moreover, if they could build it on their own they would not have ventured through these treacherous waters to come to Africa.

Henry said black people in Africa and American are thoroughly brainwashed by the Europeans to believe that this version of the history of the world is irrefutable. He pointed out one fallacy of European history that claimed that Christopher Columbus discovered America. He asked laughingly, "How can Columbus discover America when American Indians already lived there for hundreds of years?" He said nobody could discover a place where millions of people have lived for hundreds of years. Henry said the appropriate historical interpretation could be that Columbus was the first European to discover America.

Brother Henry taught that the father of medicine was not the so-called Greek Hippocrates but a black man in Egypt called Imhotep. He taught Kwame that the whole concept of Christianity was copied from the ancient Egyptian writings, and many passages of the Bible were literally taken from the black writings on the walls of the Egyptian pyramids. Henry mentioned that there have been many instances of the so-called virgin birth in ancient history thousands of years before modern Christianity was born. Henry continued by saying that there has been many crucified saviors in Egypt for thousands of years before the Christian era.

Brother Henry said the slave master is clever and good at stealing other people's writings and information to contort them to mislead the masses so he can dominate and exploit them. Henry advised that if black people would search for their own truths and get away from foreign educational propaganda, they would discover that they are indeed great people and can combine their strength to build a new African civilization on the continent of Africa.

He concluded that black Americans and Africans are the same people, divided by the slave master or the colonialist to prevent them from creating a new civilization that would be unparallel on earth.

Henry added that the sad part of modern propaganda education is that these Africans and black Americans are taught every thing about European philosophers like Francis Bacon, Voltaire, Herbert Spencer, Immanuel Kant, Schopenhauer, Fredrich Nietzsche, but nothing about African philosophers or the wisdom distilled in African proverbs. He continued that Africans are ridiculed as an inferior species in many of these universities, and because of the incessant, consistent, and systematic negativities about Africa that permeate modern education, the recipients of such information begin to look down upon Africans. He added that the black people unconsciously begin to accept their inferior status in society.

Henry concluded that this makes them look down upon their own people, who have not had the benefit of this so-called education. He described Kwame's education and experience in white Missouri as a cesspool that needs to be cleaned off him so he can be useful to his people.

Brother Henry continued to preach to Kwame that both Africans and black Americans who study political science, economics, sociology, and business administration study the slave master's methods and systems of development, which are inapplicable in many instances to the African situation. He said African and black students are not taught that African societies have experimented with various forms of governments and societal arrangements for thousands of years, and that Africans practiced cooperative democracy for thousands of years before the arrival of the Europeans.

He added that African governments are in such deplorable condition because these brainwashed Western-educated Africans insist on copying European and American systems of government instead of going back to using what had efficiently worked in Africa for thousands of years. Henry emphasized that the sad aspect of this one-sided propaganda education is that many Africans and black Americans are trained to come out of these colleges and universities with arms full of degrees and claim, "Master, see me now. I am as smart as you are. Now please give me a job so I can become exactly as you are." He added that if these educated people cannot find jobs in their field of study, which they seldom find, they become disillusioned. He said these educated people become of little use to their people, because if they were truly educated, then they could think for themselves; develop joint ventures with their brothers in America and Africa to establish businesses to hire their own people.

He said, "Look at the example of the Chinese and how progressive they are in America with Chinese foods. Or look at the Koreans who are new immigrants to America, or the Vietnamese, or the Arabs in America with their small grocery stores. Now, Kwame tell me what prevents the black American or the African from emulating these shinning examples?" Brother Henry educated Kwame to know that, because these black Americans are going around with arms full of degrees, begging for the white man's jobs, they consider the incoming Africans as their competitors and become hostile to them, and vice versa.

Henry said the black Africans behave the same as the American black, because the African believes deeply that the colonialist government and economic systems they studied like parrots at the various universities and colleges will help solve their present predicament on the African continent. Henry continued to say that the colonialist system was designed for the exploitation of the Africans and that its wholesale implementation by Africans will never succeed in developing Africa. He said the Africans' continued insistence on copying this alien systems is at the root of the current malaise in Africa and these failed alien policies are fuelling the exodus of Africans escaping the resulting grinding poverty by going to America and looking for safe havens, which the black American finds threatening.

Brother Henry challenged Kwame to take a look at his own country, Ghana, where Dr. Busia, an Oxford professor and a one-time prime minister of Ghana, was so brainwashed that he begged the colonialists in Britain to delay Ghana's freedom. He said that Ghana was not ready for its freedom in 1957 and that the freedom should be delayed until Ghanaians were ready!

"Tell me," Henry inquired, "how sick can a man be to actually beg his master not to grant him his freedom after hundreds of years of servitude?" Brother Henry emphasized that Busia's messed-up attitude and behavior was like some of the educated Negro here in America who clings tightly to his master—so much so that when the master is sick he cries and says, "Master, we are sick," and when the master is hungry he says, "Master, we are hungry." Henry continued to say that such scholars are merely walking echoes of their masters; and these people are really the problems of the black race because they foster the division and the underdevelopment of the entire black race. Henry reemphasized that the vast majority of the black masses know absolutely nothing about Africa, but the problem is that their leaders, the so-called Negroes' or Uncle Tom's leadership who are deliberately handpicked by the slave master, are misleading their people because they are furthering the slave master's interest.

Brother Henry confessed that as much as many black Americans adore Kwame Nkrumah, Ghana's founding father, he never looked critically at the Ghanaian society's rich traditional and cultural institutions to set up a government that would incorporate some of these practices, particularly the century-old cooperative democratic system all over the rural areas of Ghana. He said instead Kwame Nkrumah literally made himself into an Osagyefo, a messiah or a tyrant, and coerced his people to sycophantically worship him. Brother Henry laughed loudly and jokingly surmised that Kwame Nkrumah was so messed up and confused by his Western propaganda education that he did not even find beauty in his own Ghanaian or black American women, and so he had to marry one of those secondhand white people, his avowed Arab enemy from faraway Egypt. Henry said this confusion of the educated class in Africa and black America to undermine their people is what is responsible for the nightmare of our race today.

Kwame asked Brother Henry if he believed, as many black Americans claim, that the Africans sold the blacks into slavery. He answered by saying that this is the master trickster talking again to deceive the world by blaming the victim for the evil deeds of the slave master and the colonialist. "Hey, very soon they will be saying the Africans should be blamed for colonialism and imperialism, when Europeans stole their lands and mineral and agricultural resources." He said the truth about slavery is found with the Arabs—nobody but the Arabs—who were busy fighting from North Africa to all parts of the continent to carry slaves to the white man on the coast.

Brother Henry educated Kwame that blacks once peopled the entire continent of Africa, and the Sahara desert was a fertile forest region with lakes throughout.

He said the problem with the African is that he is too trusting of people, and that is his downfall. The African should learn not to be too trusting, too friendly, easy to laugh with strangers, easy to accommodate strangers and aliens, and too quick to foolishly share what he has.

Henry reminded Kwame about the sad story of the Cameroonian student he mentioned to him earlier, who was killed in Missouri by a stranger. He said the student was killed because of his African tradition of been too trusting, too friendly, and too accommodating of strangers.

He advised Africans to get away from being too trusting of aliens, because the Arab got a foothold on the continent of Africa because Africans were too trusting and never questioned the motives of strangers.

Henry concluded that when the Arabs came from Arabian deserts to Africa, they were accepted with open hands, and over hundreds of years these Arabs became a formidable foe of the Africans. This dangerous foe began systematically driving the Africans southward until all North Africa became predominantly Arabs, and then they moved menacingly to sell the remnants of the blacks living among them to the Europeans.

The Arabs continued to pillage African villages, destroy them, and sell the captured Africans into slavery.

Brother Henry said, "Look at what the Arab is doing in the Sudan today: a continual downward move and destruction and pillaging of the black race, while they occupy their lands."

He concluded in his own words that the "slave trade would never have taken place, and blacks would not have been in America but for the wickedness of the foul, rotten, low-down Arabs."

Brother Henry eventually finished by making the following observations:

- Kwame, I am extremely proud of what you are attempting to do and your mindset to accomplish your goals, because many, many Africans throughout the years have come to America to go to school, get a job, get married, and in time get old, retire, and die. Most of their knowledge never truly benefits the masses of the African people. I was emotionally overwhelmed when you began firing those blunt questions at me. Then I knew you were a different brother from the continent, interested in the affairs and betterment of our African race. Whatever you eventually come to do, make our people understand that world politics is nothing but the great issue of the various races' determination to dominate, subjugate, and exploit the so-called weaker races.

- I am a black American and you are an African, but we have the same strong black blood coursing through our veins. But other races have worked almost overtime to divide, dominate, and exploit our race for their enrichment; and they have succeeded by using any means possible to divide our race for continuing exploitation. Do not be discouraged as you talk to both black Americans and Africans, because the relentless propaganda warfare to divide our race will be made clear to you in the hostile responses used to denigrate each other.

- Whatever you do, please mention that the African race has inculcated certain weak values and moral beliefs that make them easy prey of other races, and this has brought about the misery and downfall of our race. Some of the feminine values I can remember are: the African is too nice and decent to ensure his own survival in this wicked world; he is too trusting of strangers and other races so he becomes an easy prey for other races. The African is too lenient and understanding and easily forgives other peoples' misdeeds against him. The African erroneously believes that good deeds, kindness, turning the other cheek, humbleness, docility, meekness, good-heartedness, gentleness, humaneness, and God-fearing qualities will guarantee him a front row seat in God's heaven. But the African must know he is here on planet earth at this level of his existence and must learn, like all other races have done, to safeguard his existence here first, before he can imagine some faraway heaven. If the African cannot safeguard his existence here on earth, how can he storm the heavens? The African should remember that God has given dominion of this planet to the strongest, and those that survive do the will of God. The will of God is what the Israelites did in their sojourn from slavery in Egypt throughout the wilderness by fighting fiercely, without regard to any morality, to conquer all their enemies. The Almighty God will be angry with the African for allowing other races to abuse him on a planet over which he has given dominion to him and all other people.

- The African race should immediately adopt and emulate the mean-spirited, aggressive, hostile values, and bullheadedness of the conquering races. It should adopt the inner constitution of the lion or the tiger in the jungle, because this planet has become a jungle and only the strong survive. The scientific method of race domination has always been through aggressive warfare, like the Israelis in the Middle East, Americans against the Indians, Julius Caesar expanding the Roman Empire, Chairman Mao's long march to unify poverty-stricken China into a world power, the Japanese during World War II, the British in their global march to dominate the world, and the aggressiveness of other races that have dominated the earth. You see no nonsense approach to politics of the young leader in Ghana, Jerry John Rawlings? This is what is vitally needed in Africa. If Africa had five Jerry Rawlings, the entire continent would change from its present confusion and malaise into a strong, powerful place, and perhaps at least West Africa could unite into one giant country for the benefit of the entire region.

• Please remind Africans not to believe or take to heart the lies in the Bible about turning the other cheek, meekness inheriting the earth, giving all your promises to God because God will provide, loving thy neighbor as thyself; doing unto others as you would want done unto you, giving all your wealth to the poor, and other values that the slave master and the colonialist preach but do not practice. These insane values were deliberately designed to keep the African docile and easily exploited. The African must wake up and throw the chains of slavery into the eyes of his enemy by adopting the values of the conquering races.

- If the Africans do not wake up to employ the aggressive, masculine, domineering, and conquering attitudes of other races, the entire African continent will be overrun and the African will be made a slave again in his own homeland. The African people will be destroyed by the wicked machinations of the conquering races, who would deliberately manufacture diseases, famine, and engineer warfare to destroy the so-called peace-loving people on the continent, making room for another conquering race to occupy it. They would do this because of their envy of and greedy desire for the still untapped wealth of Africa.

FOUR

FINALLY, TOWARD THE END OF 1983 Ms. Roxanna Pearson, who had been in constant communication with Kwame, moved from upstate New York to join him in New York City to concretize the details of the research work they had undertaken during the previous three years.

When they began working in the early days of 1984, they fell in love and tied the knot on April 21, 1984 in the crowded People's Community Baptist Church in Buffalo, New York, where many Africans and black American well-wishers witnessed the happy occasion. The couple remains married to this day (in 2006).

The couple, writing as joint authors, refers to themselves throughout the rest of the book as "we."

OUR ENCOUNTER IN SPANISH HARLEM

Our first interview in New York City began in the Spanish Harlem, where we met an old black American schoolteacher who belonged to several black organizations in Harlem and had written children's books to help elevate the self-esteem of black boys in America. Her name was Christine, and because of her many years of teaching we affectionately referred to her, as her school children did, as Ms. Christine.

We asked Ms. Christine what she thought the problem between the Africans and black Americans was. We wanted to know why many black Americans appear to look condescendingly upon the Africans as inferior beings. We wanted to find out why many black people instinctively have superior attitudes toward the African, why they laugh and make funny jokes about the African when he talks, and generally what makes even the most ignorant and illiterate black American feel that he is better and knows more than the most educated African he meets.

Ms. Christine—a well-educated, honest, and straight-talking lady who does not bite her tongue when she speaks—began by telling us that the white man knew that Africans were coming to America and he carefully designed a master plan to prepare for their arrival.

Ms. Christine continued by saying that the white man saw that the African countries were becoming independent and that their sons and daughters would struggle to receive their education abroad, particularly in America, the most economically, financially, technologically, and politically developed nation in the world. Ms. Christine said America even helped speed up the decolonization process and gave enormous financial assistance, including scholarships, to the best and the brightest sons and daughters of Africa to be educated in America to gain the upper hand against the their then bitter rival, the defunct Union of Soviet Socialist Republics (USSR). Ms. Christine continued to reveal that the master plan was to continue the age-old shrewd policy of divide and conquer. "In this plan," she explained, "the white man covered all his bases tightly without allowing any loopholes for both the Africans and the black Americans to see his modus operandi." She revealed that the first base was through entertainments, with the help of Hollywood.

Here, the white man created a fictitious, humorous, tree-swinging Tarzan, his beautiful seductress wife Jane, and their pet cheetah and deliberately placed them in the so-called jungles of Africa. She added that the white man cleverly, shrewdly, and deliberately portrayed the native Africans in several villages as half-naked, ignorant, primitive, barbaric, ugly, ape-looking with painted faces, mumbling some mumbo-jumbo words to each other.

Ms. Christine further revealed that these native Africans were caricatured as fierce, dangerous, spear-carrying people dwelling in backward huts surrounded by dirty flies and unsanitary conditions. The Africans were further portrayed as cannibals who make wild fires and drummed and danced around them while cooking a human being in a big pot on top, singing, and acting like buffoons.

They sang a deliberately concocted imbecilic-sounding song like "wayaa yoo, wayaa yoo, yoo yoo, bubu bubu, mungu mungu, buana, ongwa, yeyeyoooo." Occasionally these half-naked, barbaric, and ugly primitive Africans were depicted as savages who attacked each other and sometimes would kidnap Tarzan's wife; and miraculously Tarzan would swing on the jungle trees, kill some of the primitive Africans, and rescue his wife Jane. These fictitious Tarzan movies were repeatedly shown on television as the staple movie in America on almost daily basis on one channel or another. This was the white man's clever depiction of Africa to the black American. Ms. Christine said, "You can imagine the powerful effect these propaganda movies had on the innocent black American."

She continued, "Many black Americans from infancy to adulthood were bombarded with these negative and primitive images of Africa. This constant and repeated brainwashing and powerful propaganda warfare is what black Americans were subjected to in America over decades."

She said these negative images of Africa and Africans were deeply etched, or embedded, in the subconscious of many black Americans. This deliberate and cleverly constructed propaganda warfare distorted the image black Americans in general had about their brothers and sisters in Africa. She said these powerful images of Africa and Africans formed a greater part of the black American's perception of Africa.

Ms. Chritine said you could not blame the black American, who had never been to Africa to see that these images were blatant deceptions meant to deceive him. She compared this powerful propaganda warfare to the experiment of Ivan Petrovich Pavlov, the Russian psychiatrist who experimented with dogs by ringing a bell and feeding them, until they were conditioned to associate the bell ringing with food. The next time the bell rang; saliva oozed out of the dogs, even though no food was given to the dogs, because the repeated bell ringing and feeding had classically and cognitively conditioned the dogs.

Ms. Christine said that in the same clever manner, the repeated horrible propaganda technique of deliberately portraying negative images of Africans as savages, barbaric, half-naked, primitive, cannibals running wild in the African jungle with spears and swinging on trees had conditioned black Americans to cognitively perceive Africa and Africans as such. Christine informed us that as we interview many black Americans, these deliberate propaganda images that are indelibly etched in their consciousness; they are what many blacks would likely tell us, she said.

Christine said the propaganda warfare against Africans did not end with these deliberate Hollywood pernicious caricature of Africans; it went another step forward to include numerous educational television documentation designed and powerfully narrated by serious intellectuals and academic scholars trained in some of the best universities in America and England.

She maintained that these documentaries further accentuated the pernicious propaganda warfare against Africans. Almost all of the documentaries depicted only the negative, poverty-stricken, disease-infected areas and tribal warfare in the deep, impenetrable jungles of Africa. Ms. Christine stressed that these powerful propaganda documentaries against Africa deliberately overplayed almost on daily basis the negative and grotesque images of Africa to the world.

Ms. Christine continued to emphasize that if the white man was not involved in hostile propaganda against the African; he would have been intellectually honest and would have balanced the images depicted in many of the documentaries about Africa.

She added that a true and intellectually honest portrayal of Africa (like anywhere else in the world) would be to show both the negative and positive images of the African continent. She added that any observer watching one of these hostile propaganda documentaries about Africa that in most cases only depict wild animals, savage and uncivilized people inhabiting the continent, is led to conclude that Africa is indeed a backward continent. She said an observer is led to believe that there are no modern buildings, paved roads, or foreign embassies (including many United States consular offices spread around all the black countries in Africa).

She continued to reveal that these documentaries deliberately refuse to show modern African cities with teeming populations of millions, like Lagos, Abuja, Accra, Abidjan, Dakar, Lome, Douala, Nairobi, Kampala, Entebbe, and other African cities. Ms. Christine said if the Africans were as hostile and conniving as the white man is, they would also deliberately ignore the greatness of America and only show their people who have never been to America documentaries of the blighted neighborhoods in America. She added Africans can depict in their documentaries the destroyed, poverty-stricken, crime-ridden, and dangerous areas like Harlem, East St. Louis, Appalachia, South Central Los Angeles and its gangsters and hoodlums with their guns and graffitists, the Mississippi Delta, and some unpaved roads in Arkansas, Mississippi, and South Carolina. She added that such deliberate propaganda would lead Africans to conclude that America is as violent and underdeveloped as the documentaries portray it.

Ms. Christine continued to say that the relentless propaganda assault against Africa did not end with these negative documentaries, but almost all schools and colleges textbooks, national and regional magazines, periodicals, newspapers, and even scholarly journals continue to depict Africa as primitive, backward, undeveloped, disease-infected, and dangerous.

She exclaimed that they even described Africa as the 'dark continent' and made it their business to preach the false notion of African inferiority, ignorance, backwardness, and savagery, depicting it as a place of "jungle-bunnies" swinging on trees to innocent, impressionistic, and naive students, from their infancy, through primary and high schools, to the university level!

Ms. Christine concluded that this deliberate, persistent, and systematic societal conditioning, or socialization, of black Americans about Africa from their infancy to adulthood has made many black Americans perceive Africans as backward and inferior people.

She supported her conclusion by referring to Charles Reich's book, *The Greening of America*, which states, "Consciousness is in substantial degree socially determined…included in the idea of consciousness is a person's background, education, politics, insights, values, emotions, and philosophy…it is the whole man; his head; his way of life."1

Ms. Christine further supported her assertion by noting that Zig Ziglar, the motivational speaker from Texas, revealed that, "You are what you are because of what goes into your mind… The pictures those words represent get into our heads, and have strong effect on the way we think." 2

Ms. Christine continued to reinforce and emphasize that people's perceptions, attitudes, outlooks, and beliefs are shaped and, "the stories we tell and are told mold our perceptions of reality." 3

Ms. Christine added that black American consciousness, or their perception of Africa, is the result of systematic and persistent brainwashing through their movies, their schools, magazines, and the lies they are told about Africa.

Ms. Christine repeated that these negative stories in Tarzan movies, together with the negative pictures in the documentaries and negative stories about Africa have molded their perceptions, attitudes, beliefs, and outlooks about Africa and African peoples. Ms. Christine concluded that the cumulative effects of the deliberate, hostile propaganda warfare against the African are:

- Many black Americans generally look down upon Africans as inferior beings. Some even believe that welfare recipients, drug addicts, illiterates, and convicts are better off than the most educated and sophisticated African. Essentially, they perceive Africans as savage, barbaric, primitive, and inferior people, and do not want to associate with them.

- Some really believe that Africans are unclean, uncivilized, less intelligent, and that they stink, since they dwell in caves, forests, and surrounded by animals.

- Many black Americans generally laugh and make fun of the African when he speaks with an accent. Some ignorant blacks refer to the accents as talking funny. Some blacks, including the poorly educated, believe that Africans do not speak properly and therefore, do not know what they are saying. The irony is that some blacks who speak Ebonics attempt to "correct" the King's English that most Africans speak by forming it into their Ebonics expressions, which are filled with unconjugated verbs. The sad fact is that these same black Americans listen attentively to Europeans or Spanish or Russians speak English with their foreign accents, and admire them.

- Some black Americans even make fun of African names and deliberately pronounce those names jokingly to poke fun at the different sounds in the names. But these same black people will not dare do that to Italian, Polish, or the difficult Eastern European names.

- Some children born of African parentage who have been conditioned or negatively socialized about the daily negativities of Africa show some degree of condescension toward their African parents. Some are ashamed that their parents are Africans, others disrespect their African parents, and yet some do not want to identify with Africans and so change their African names to that of the slave master's.

- The sad part is that some black American women who marry or befriend Africans unconsciously believe that they are superior to their African men; therefore, they treat them in demeaning and derogatory ways—ways that they dare not behave around black American men. Essentially most of these black ladies boss their African men around.

- Some blacks still believe that Africa is one country, and some do not know the names of any independent country in Africa, and it would be an awesome task for any of them to name one city in black Africa.

- But surprisingly a great deal of black Americans have transcended, overcome, and seen through the lies in this hostile propaganda warfare against the African. Some of these blacks are more Afro-centric than many Africans, some have established African poetry and dance theatres, some have begun visiting many African countries, and some are trading and establishing professional relationships with Africans in America and those on the continent. A small number have moved permanently to resettle in African countries. By and large, there is a growing trend of black Americans gradually discovering their African roots, and a variety of black churches are sponsoring vital missions, hospitals, clinics, and chartering schools all over Africa. Some black philanthropists and millionaires are donating millions of dollars in support of a variety of health-related projects in Africa.

Ms. Christine ended by telling us that, "as you approach and interview most of these black Americans about Africa, you should not be surprised that most of their responses will gravitate toward their negative perceptions and imagery about Africa and Africans, but watch out for the few enlightened and well-traveled blacks who have transcended this propaganda against Africans."

And to gain a better understanding, we questioned the ordinary black Americans about the true beliefs, feelings, and perceptions that they have about their brothers and sisters in Africa. We wanted to know how they developed these attitudes and perceptions about Africa.

Our intrusive questionnaires were designed to find out how they relate, perceive, or react toward the incoming Africans, and conversely, how the Africans also react to the black Americans.

FIVE

A SIXTY-FIVE-YEAR-OLD BLACK MAN, BILL from Homer, Louisiana, informed us that Africans should realize that they are coming to America, where black Americans has been abused and segregated and have gone through all kinds of hellish treatment from the slave master.

He said black Americans fought, bled, and died to get most of the Civil Rights Act of 1964 passed through Congress, a bill that ultimately outlawed segregation. Bill continued to tell us that blacks fought tooth and nail in America to ensure that most schools and colleges became integrated and admitted black people.

He insisted that many black Americans resent the Africans when they come in here to America to take advantage of all the benefits of these hard-fought struggles without acknowledging the efforts of the black American.

Bill said, "Many of these incoming Africans do not freely mingle or make concerted attempts to talk with the blacks, and many seem arrogant to us." He said the blacks perceive the Africans as arrogant, unfriendly, unapproachable, and people who move about with blank expressions on their faces. He continued to say that many of them are not warm, embracive, and nice to the black Americans. "And some even act like their shit doesn't stink."

Bill added that the negative and unfriendly attitudes of many Africans make the average black American uncomfortable around the African.

He said that some Africans erroneously believe that many of the average black Americans are lazy, on drugs, not motivated enough to go to college, and only want to collect welfare checks from Uncle Sam. He said in every society there are some members of the population who are struggling and need government help, but a greater majority of black Americans are hardworking people.

Bill told us that the negative perceptions and stereotypes some Africans have been brainwashed to believe about the blacks create unnecessary hostility and serve to separate them.

Bill, however, admitted that many Africans who come to America are forced to discipline themselves to work hard to become self-employed by opening up stores, driving taxis, exporting and importing all kinds of merchandise, and entering into other lucrative business ventures to become successful. He added that some black Americans want these same achievements or accomplishments but cannot or refuse to discipline themselves to attain these goals. And, therefore, they resent the Africans and their achievements in America.

Bill concluded that many Africans coming to a new country sometimes become timid or fearful or apprehensive to approach the black Americans because of the lies or myths or the pervasive propaganda against the black Americans by the media or the white society and what they might have heard from other Africans.

He said many Africans become so "snowed" by this propaganda against the blacks that they begin to fear the blacks and such timidity and fear creates a huge barrier between them.

He added that many Africans tend to stick to themselves and have their small country-based organizations or even tribal-based groups, and they seldom reach out to the numerous black organizations, associations, clubs, churches, agencies, businesses, and other activities that are proliferating all over this great nation. He said many Africans do not get involved with the black society; hence, they do not know about the various opportunities available to them in the black communities and businesses.

He said there are many predominantly black American senior citizens centers in New York City, but seldom do you find many of these African senior citizens participating and accessing the many benefits available at these senior centers, because many do not reach out of their little tribal clicks that continue to imprison them even in a great, diversified, and pluralistic society like America.

BROTHER AL.FROM MIAMI

A middle-aged man Brother Al from Miami, Florida told us that Africans do not recognize that the black American is undergoing posttraumatic slave syndrome, which makes him behave and act the way he does. He said the ordeal that blacks went through during slavery and its aftermath was a horrible, traumatic experience beyond description.

He said modern people couldn't conceptualize the horrible abuses and trauma that the black American endured—the horrible separation from loved ones; mass raping of innocent, vulnerable black teenagers nicknamed wenches by the slave masters and sons, the untold barbaric and inhuman lashings on the bare backs of the slaves, the branding of slaves with a hot iron to distinguish them from the various masters, the life of working like mules from sunup till sundown, the numerous inhuman lynchings, and a countless other inhuman and barbaric treatments of the slaves.

Brother Al added that, apart from the physical abuse and terror meted to the slaves, there was also the damage done to their psyche. The black Americans were forced to reject their African heritage. Those who spoke their African language were mercilessly whipped or mutilated so they would stop, and their African names were deliberately taken away from them and substituted with slave names, like Kinta Kunte in Roots was forcefully changed to Tobi.

Brother Al also reminded us that the slaves were deliberately kept ignorant, preventing them from learning to read and write. In most cases if a slave was caught reading, the punishment was death or cutting off his tongue and some limbs.

Brother Al told us that the slaves were made to believe that God created them to be slaves of the white man and they should accept their place as slaves. He said it was impressed upon the slaves that they were less intelligent human beings and so they were to be perpetually the hewers of wood and drawers of water for their masters.

Brother Al said the slave masters designed a whole catalog of literature meant to prove the inferiority of the black race and the superiority of their masters. Brother Al said in time some of the slaves began to believe that maybe what the slave masters were teaching them could be true and they began to take these teaching to heart. He said what the black American has undergone in American is a horrible, traumatic experience, and therefore, many are not truly adjusted to living or coexisting peacefully with the slave master.

He said if you couple this traumatic experience of the black American with segregation, Jim Crowism, the continuing institutional racism, subtle ostracism from mainstream America, and the continuing police profiling of black males, then the incoming Africans could begin to understand the horrible daily stresses that the average black American undergoes in this country. He said this posttraumatic stress syndrome is responsible for much of the sabotage that the blacks appear to deliberately inflict upon themselves and each other. He said when the Africans see many blacks not educating themselves but acting in self-destructive ways, they should understand that the blacks are going through posttraumatic slave {stress} syndrome and desperately need help. Brother Al said Africans should not be quick to judge these black Americans without understanding how they have evolved in this country.

He added that the ancestors of these black Americans worked as slaves with no monetary compensation to build America and create the capital or financial base for the subsequent economic development that took place in America. He said the children of the slave masters have developed to become millionaires, and some billionaires, from the sweat on the brows of these black Americans.

Brother Al said it is morally unacceptable for a Christian country like America to refuse to make restitution to the sons and daughters of the African slaves that built America. He said the Japanese who were falsely put in barbed-wire camps during World War II have received reparation payments; the Jews have received some form of reparation payments for their sufferings and loss of properties under the odious hands of the lunatic and bloodthirsty Adolf Hitler.

He challenged the incoming Africans to pressure their governments to put the issue of reparation payments to black Americans at the United Nations so it can be debated in the international forum to pressure our governments to make financial restitution to black Americans. Brother Al said his only fear is that black Americans might use all of their reparation payments to buy SUVs and Cadillacs, giving the money right back to the slave masters' children.

A LADY FROM FLORENCE, SOUTH CAROLINA

We spoke to a black lady, Alice from Florence, South Carolina, who told us that when she hears Africans talk with their foreign accents, her first impression is that they talk funny because they do not understand the English language well. Our minds have been trained to hear what good English speech sounds like, and not the mumbo jumbo we hear Africans speak.

She said many black Americans like herself know deep down in their hearts that they are better or superior to the African. She continued, "We have been taught to know what the standards and sense of beauty are, and Africans with their kinky hair, thick noses, and ugly facial features are definitely not our sense of beauty, so we do not see Africans as beautiful."

She continued to inform us that blacks have been trained to look down upon the African as a "jungle bunny" by the numerous negative movies, documentaries, and books about Africa.

Alice said whites have trained and conditioned black Americans in their magazines, books, newspapers, and television programs to believe that Africans are backward and inferior and that black people should learn to disassociate themselves from Africans and look up to Europeans as their only models of success.

She continued to say that when black Americans see an African, they picture dense jungles with half-naked Africans living around monkeys. She swore that these negative perceptions of Africa continue to dominate the mindset of black Americans to this day.

When we asked Alice whether she likes to go back to Africa, she responded, "How can I go back to a place I have never been to?" She also said that she sees many Africans coming to America to stay. "So how can I even consider going to a place that the natives are running away from?" she said.

We also asked her to name any African city but she could not.

Finally, when asked to make any general observation about Africa and Africans, she said, "Africa has been set up to be like a country with poor hygiene. Whenever I see many of these African girls in Harlem braiding people's hair, I wonder whether they have had their shots or inoculations. I certainly do not want them to touch my hair for fear that they are filthy and can transmit some disease to me."

She said whenever her daughters go to the African women in Harlem to get their hair braided, she warns them not to touch cups or even go to her kitchen until they wash their hair with antiseptic soaps, for fear of disease contaminating the kitchen.

When asked to explain to us what specifically had any African done to her personally, she responded that no African had ever done anything bad to her and said that Africans she has met have been extremely nice and helpful to her.

THE BROOKLYN WOMAN'S RESPONSE

We stubbornly and relentlessly followed black Americans, with all kinds of questions designed to discover what they think about Africa and Africans deep down in their hearts and how they came to have that mindset about Africans.

Venus—a young lady born in New York City and currently residing in Brooklyn, New York—said black Americans are definitely superior to Africans and even "welfare recipients who depend on the government for survival, and prisoners, including those pushing drugs and those not working, believe they are better off than the most sophisticated African."

She continued to say that, "We black Americans see many Africans doing menial jobs, like driving taxis with their dirty clothes, but you rarely see them in positions of authority in America."

Additionally, she continued, "When you turn on your television set all you see about Africa is their dire poverty, disgusting diseases, women with no clothes and their tits sagging out, and children with protruding bellies with all kinds of flies on their faces."

She said that those daily pictures they see about Africa convince the average black American that his condition is better than the African's and makes "us blacks view Africans as an inferior species, unable to survive on their own, running away from their warm countries to America with all our horrible winters."

An unforgettable encounter Venus related to us happened when she was nine months pregnant and she called from the hospital on a hot summer day to request for information on her insurance. The African personnel officer spoke rapidly, without waiting for her response, and hung up the phone on her. However, she confessed that an African businessman helped her find good employment with a company that is still her current employer.

THE CHICAGO MAN

A black man, Dickson from Chicago, Illinois, also added that black Americans have been indoctrinated by the white man's philosophy into his way of thinking and therefore perceive Africans in a condescending manner. He also reminded us that many black Americans also believe that the African is arrogant and has a superiority complex.

He said their arrogance comes from the way they speak and their rudeness to the black American. Dickson added that "the

African shows off by down talking to the blacks in a condescending tonality."

He indicated to us that one day he was in an African man's store and wanted to buy something, but the storekeeper looked at him like he was there to steal something and spoke rudely and condescendingly to him. That made him uncomfortable.

A NOTE FROM SELMA, ALABAMA

An eighty-year-old woman, Sarah from Selma, Alabama, who marched during the civil rights movement with Rev. Martin Luther King, Jr. from Selma to Montgomery, Alabama, reminded us that black Americans came from Africa, no matter how many of them may want to deny that fact.

She said after the demise of overt segregation in America, the integration they achieved further divided black Americans into different classes: the successful and the downtrodden, struggling masses of black people (or the haves and the have-nots).

She said the successful black Americans moved to suburbs, where the white middle class lives, while the vast majorities of the poor and nearly poor were left in the ghettos of inner cities of America.

She said the highly successful blacks in corporate America have little interaction with the incoming Africans, but ironically some of these uppity blacks are more likely to travel to Africa because of their intellectual curiosity.

She continued to add that some of these upper-class blacks provide some useful and valuable services to the impoverished African masses; some have missions to minister to the sick and needy Africans, some donate pharmaceutical products and food to feed many African people, while some donate large sums of money to help Africans establish schools and other worthwhile products.

She continued to inform us that some of these upper-class blacks form partnerships with highly Westernized Africans to exploit the wealth of Africa. Sarah further explained that some of these black professionals unfortunately become Uncle Toms and pretend to love Africans by mingling with Africans only to spy on them for their slave master.

She said many of these black spies are spread all over the African continent, and it would behoove Africans to learn to keep an eye on these Uncle Toms. Sarah revealed that the overwhelming majority of these upper-class blacks not only look condescendingly upon the vast majority of the struggling masses of black Americans, but also fear them and in many cases refuse to interact with them.

She revealed that the vast majority of Africans coming to America are more likely to interact with the masses of the dispossessed black Americans who are fiercely discriminated upon in America and therefore feel they are in competition with these incoming Africans.

She added that these incoming Africans are trying to adjust to a new land and have many problems with language, employment, and immigration authorities; and the best black Americans can do is not add to their problems but leave them alone or help them adjust to American life. She informed us that black Americans are like crabs in a barrel and are jealous and envious of each other, particularly those who are succeeding financially.

She added that many of the masses of the have-nots in black America erroneously assume that Africans get a lot of financial help from the American government when they arrive here in America; therefore, they become resentful of the Africans.

Sarah concluded that many Africans she has met are hardworking, like many black Americans, and are determined to succeed in their adopted land. She advised that many Africans cannot afford to live in the neighborhoods where the upper-class live, so they are all confined to low- to middle- class areas or the ghettoes, where they mix and mingle with black Americans.

She finally said that Africans' experience in America is colored by their interactions with predominantly the masses of black America and not necessarily the upper-middle class of blacks. Therefore, what they say about blacks mainly pertains to the masses of the average, struggling black Americans.

REV. HOPES OF NEW YORK CITY

Once again we were privileged to get the opportunity to interview a powerful minister, Rev. Hopes from New York City. The Rev. Hopes emphatically told us that Africans should definitely be respected because they are the mothers and fathers of black Americans. He told us that there are educated Africans and black Americans, and there are illiterate and ignorant ones.

He further told us that the seemingly great difference between the black Americans and Africans is the result of a big ignorance. He said this ignorance is fomented by the slave master to prosper and profit by this mental ignorance of our race—of who they truly are and the immense historical contributions they have made to modern civilization.

He added that "once our people are kept in ignorance, it is easy to keep them in perpetual subjection and to have absolute power over them, because power concedes absolutely nothing without demand. It never did and never will."

Reverend Hopes informed us that if he had listened to the lies and myths he was indoctrinated with at school about how savage and barbaric African people were; it would have affected his own self-image. He said many black Americans who believe in the lies and myths of the slave master about black Americans and Africans have developed a low self-image, which leads them to all kinds of self-destructive behavior, like alcoholism, substance abuse, deliberate neglect of their children, or calling their women all kinds of horrible names. He reminded us that most black Americans grew up believing that dark skin was a bad thing and the foolishness that Tarzan was the king of the jungle; such negativities contribute to black self-hatred, self-destruction, and being resentful of each other. He reminded us that the pervasiveness of black-on-black crime has its genesis in black self-hatred, because of the negative propaganda warfare perpetrated against the entire black race.

Rev. Hopes reminded us that Africans do not necessarily understand what the black Americans have been through in America and therefore do not understand why blacks behave the way they do. He said black Americans have been indoctrinated to go to the Europeans for an education, to beg them for jobs, to worship their gods, and to let black children look up to them.

He reminded us again that black Americans have been treated inhumanely and abusively for many, many years by the slave master and have allowed themselves to be brainwashed that they are nothing and will not amount to anything in this world. He added that in schools their teachers had low expectations of them, and they were discouraged from being top lawyers, doctors, or senators but were encouraged to learn a trade or do menial work because that was what God intended for the black race.

He said because of years of ingrained oppression, coupled with persistent and systematic negative propaganda against the self-image of the black American, the black American has become angry and violent, self-destructive and quick to anger. He reminded us that the black American situation has become a vicious cycle because of their self-destructiveness and quick tempers. And so the Europeans use fierce violence and excessive force to subdue and control them. Rev. Hopes asked us to remember what happened to an unarmed West African immigrant, Amadu Diallo, who was shot thirty-two times by four New York City police officers who swore they were only defending themselves from him. He added, "And the mighty white judge believed them and set them free!"

He said that both the black American and the African had better learn to work together or they will perish together. He finally said, "Both the African and the black American must learn their true history, and teach it to their children, and let them know that they were the cradle of civilization and of creation itself. And this power of knowing the truth will dispel the horrible negative propaganda we have been exposed to."

He advised that every black American must visit Africa at least once in his lifetime to reconnect with his ancestors, and shake off some of the mythology and lies about Africa and Africans.

He concluded by saying that both black Americans and Africans must know and be proud of the fact that the Almighty God chose them first in his creation to have dominion over the earth, but they have let this awesome opportunity slip away to other races that are currently abusing the black race. He supported his assertion that the black race was God's chosen people from the Bible. He quoted that in Genesis 1:26 it is written, "And God said, Let us make man in our image, after our likeness." And in Genesis 1:27 it is written, "So God created man in his own image, in the image of God created he him." Then in Genesis 2:7 it is written, "And the Lord God formed man of the DUST of the ground..."

Rev. Hopes emphasized that the color of dust is not white but either brown or black, which is the color of the black race; and since God made man in his own image, what color is God then?

A QUICK RESPONSE FROM STATEN ISLAND, NEW YORK

We proceeded to ask a lady, Maria from Staten Island, New York, whether she refers to herself as black or African American. She responded that she likes to refer to herself as a woman of color because she has different heritages mixed together. She confided to us, "I know my roots are in Africa if I trace them, but I do not feel that I am one hundred percent African, because I was not born in Africa, and I am also not one hundred percent American, because my grandfather was born in the West Indies and my grandmother was mixed up with Scottish and Irish bloods." She also indicated to us that she does not want to be called black, because it does not represent her heritage and race.

Maria told us that he thought for a long time that Africa was one country, but she later learned that it was a continent with many countries; and the only history she knew about Africa was that black slaves were brought to America by white people to work for them.

She told us that her first impression of Africa was that it was backward and underdeveloped—particularly the women. She claimed that she never saw an African woman in an academic setting, so she thought education was not important to them.

She informed us that most of her preconceived notions about Africa changed when she went to college and had a Nigerian woman as her roommate. Maria told us that she was marveled at the intelligence of her Nigerian roommate, who even helped her with most of her college homework. And she always wondered how her roommate managed to write and speak such excellent English and does mathematics and social studies so well. She admitted that many black Americans have been brainwashed by the slave master and the true history of Africa has been twisted and watered down. She added that it is extremely important for blacks to visit Africa, sit down with the tribal elders, and learn the true history of Africa.

Finally Maria confessed to us that after spending many years reading Afro-centric books on Africa, she has a great respect for Africans, because if the white man could really build America on his own, he would not have braved the mighty Atlantic Ocean to go to Africa to get them to help him develop the land that belonged to the Indians.

She added that these African people in captivity in America practically invented everything from traffic lights, to the cotton gin, discovered blood plasma, and the third rail in the subway system. She said some of the important African American inventions in America she can recall include Elijah McCoy inventing the oil-dripping cup for trains, Lewis Latimer inventing the carbon filament for light bulbs, George Washington Carver inventing peanut butter, Garrett Morgan inventing the gas mask and traffic signal, and Otis Boykin coming up with the electronic control device for guided missiles, IBM computers, and the pacemaker. She concluded that many of these Africans born in diasporas made America the great country it is today.

SERMON FROM ATLANTA, GEORGIA

The Rev. Johnson of Atlanta filled our eyes with tears as we spoke to him in his downtown office. He assured us that he did not want to put the entire blame for slavery on both the Arabs and white folks, as many Afro-centric intellectuals prefer to do. He said most of the responsibility must be borne by the Africans themselves, because most of the powerful tribal chiefs were corrupt, greedy, and ignorant, and fell for the trickery of the slave master. Rev. Johnson said that black American people who are indeed spiritual and deeply religious people must search their hearts and know the story of Joseph in the Bible and the beauty of God's work.

He told us that in Genesis 37:27 we read that Joseph was sold into slavery by his brothers, by saying, "Come and let us sell him to the Ishmaelites…then the Midianite traders passed by; so the brothers pulled Joseph up and lifted him out of the pit, and sold him to the Ishmaelites for twenty shekels of silver. And they took Joseph to Egypt."

The Rev. Johnson continued that when great famine, poverty, and hopelessness broke out in the land of Canaan, Joseph's brothers fled to Egypt to buy food to keep their bodies and souls together. And then, to their astonishment, the governor in charge of all food supplies was Joseph, the brother they sold into slavery.

The reverend said Joseph forgave his brothers and eventually filled their empty sacks with all kinds of food, fed them, and rejoiced with them. He told us to read Genesis 45:4-8:

- And Joseph said to his brothers, 'please come near to me… I am Joseph your brother, whom you sold into Egypt.
- But now, do not therefore be grieved or angry with yourselves because you sold me here for God sent me before you to preserve life.
- And God sent me before you to preserve a posterity for you in the earth, and to save your lives by a great deliverance
- So now it was not you who sent me here but God.

Reverend Johnson related the story of Joseph to the Africans and the black Americans and reminded us, among other things, that:

- The teachings of Christianity should be reflected in both Africans and black Americans—in their behavior and in how they choose to treat each other.
- Like Joseph, the Almighty God has a greater divine purpose to send black Americans all the way from the African continent to America, under such difficult, hostile, and challenging conditions.
- Today, like ancient Canaan, the entire African continent is facing horrible famine, pandemic diseases, civil instabilities, horrible early deaths at an accelerated rate, and the encroaching desertification on many arable and prime agricultural lands; and AIDS is wreaking havoc on the continent.
- Like Joseph's brothers, who sold him into slavery, our own African brothers who sold us into slavery are now fleeing their poverty-stricken, disease-infected, and hunger-prone African continent in exodus proportions to join black Americans in America, where prosperity, abundance, proper medical care, and strong military and police force that protect its citizens from harm are available.
- Therefore, as devout Christians and spirituals, as black Americans are, we have a collective divine responsibility in this gradual fulfillment of God's mighty purpose and plan. Black Americans should search deep into their hearts and thank God for what he has done to strengthen the black race by pushing blacks to sojourn in America to save the black race from the impending destruction of Africa.

- Black Americans should search their hearts and forgive their African brothers for selling them into slavery. And they should know that as much pain as blacks correctly feel, their history was an act of God, whose greater purpose transplanted them here in America.

- Hence, both the black American and the African must search their hearts to forgive each other and embrace each other, respect each other, love each other, marry each other genuinely, and work steadfastly toward uplifting of our African race.

THE SOCIAL WORKER FROM QUEENS, NEW YORK

A sixty-three-year-old woman, Margaret from Queens, New York, told us that she prefers to refer to herself as an African American because she is an African descendant living in America.

Margaret, a social worker, informed us that her first impressions about Africans were formed in her formative years in college, when she met African students. She confessed that the African students were studious and hardworking, and were mostly in the library studying. She also said that some of the African students worked full-time jobs and still maintained a full course load, and some even made the dean's list or high grade point averages. She said that while the African students were busy working and studying, many black American students like her were busy partying, getting drunk, having a good time, and making excuses for the mediocre grades.

She said some of her black friends were impressed by the way the African students stayed focused on their studies, and they emulated the African students. And she swore that she taught her own children about staying focused on their studies like those African students.

She told us that no one could categorically claim that either the African or the black American looks down upon the other. She said the way an individual behaves depends on the individual's frame of reference.

Many blacks who believe in Tarzan's movies and other negative propaganda against Africa and have not cleaned and detoxified this negative propaganda erroneously believe themselves to be superior to the Africans.

Margaret also said that some Africans erroneously look down upon black Americans, since they have succeeded in America, and wonder why the blacks who are born here cannot take advantage of the abundant opportunities available here in America. She said Africans are begging many blacks to stop using racism as a crutch or an excuse for not succeeding. She claimed that some Africans think many blacks have a victim mentality and like to blame their condition on slavery without even trying to make any effort to challenge their ingrained assumptions about the racism preventing them from succeeding.

Margaret cautioned that Africans do not realize the trauma, the abiding and continuing institutional and subtle racism still prevalent in America that prevents black Americans from achieving their goals. She further said that many Africans still do not understand the baggage and other pernicious subtle influences that continue to undermine much black American mental and emotional stability. She concluded that white Americas are more tolerant of the African presence in America, treat them fairly well, and are likelier to throw them some of their crumbs from their table, as opposed to their historically hostile treatment of the black American.

THE INCREDIBLE ROY FROM SOUTH CAROLINA

A black man named Roy from Lake City, South Carolina told us that he refers to himself as a black American because he is not from Africa; he has never been there and has virtually no desire to go there. He said he was born in America as a black man and that it is the only country he knows and cares about. And he is not an African living in America. He told us that Africa is another country where poor black people live.

He revealed that he would not even like to visit Africa, because they have too many wars, tribal fighting, a lot of contagious diseases, and profound poverty. Moreover, he informed us that he had been in battles in Korea and survived, and he does not want to be in another war or get in crossfire of bullets in Africa, since Africans like to fight most of the time. He added, "You Africans like to fight too much. You people are so violent and immature that you simply cannot get together to build your countries, but you'd rather fight and destroy the place.

Some of your leaders are corrupt. They steal and rob all the monies meant for their people. How can you Africans expect black Americans to come there with our monies to invest? I bet our monies will all be stolen by your kleptomaniacs and corrupt leaders." Roy told us that he does not have any African friends because in all his life he has not run across them, does not know any of them personally, and has not consciously made any attempt to have one as a friend, because he does not understand their culture. Roy told us that Africans think they are better than black Americans.

He thinks this because of their attitudes and the fact that they act different from the blacks. He added that the African thinks black Americans are lazy and do not want to work but rely on government welfare handouts. He said many black Americans refuse to work for little paychecks, but the African will do any work for those starvation wages the white man pays him.

He added that the Africans are coming to America in large numbers because of the starvation wages and added that black Americans feel they are too good for those meager wages.

When we challenged Roy, telling him that he had told us he had not run across any Africans and knew nothing about them. How did he arrive at all the things he was telling us about them? He answered, "That is my gut feeling about them and the way I see them. Most Africans act like we don't exist. They do not speak to us. They come from a poor country, but when they get here they act like they are better or superior to us."

LEROY'S RESPONSE FROM BOSTON

Another black American man, Leroy from Boston, Massachusetts, told us that he refers to himself as an African American because he recognizes that his forebears came from Africa and that is his heritage. He said that referring to himself as a black man is meaningless because anything can be called black; it does not relate to any heritage or ethnic origin. But to say he is an African American lets the world know that he has a line of ancestry extending all the way back to Africa, which he was proud to let the entire world know about. He said his pride in his African ancestry is deeply rooted in the fact that Africa is where it all started, including the creation of man from clay or dust, which is either black or brown and never white.

He continued to say that if the Bible is true, then Africans are the original leaders of the world and all humanity or mankind originated from them. Leroy said he had met many Africans who behaved nicely, very respectably, were well educated, and took good care of their families.

He said Africans are like all peoples of the world: Some are nice and friendly; while others can be mean and nasty. And so he refuses to lump and categorized all of them together and make a blanket statement about all of them. He said it behooves many black Americans standing on street corners and getting high on drugs and liquor to copy some of the good things they see the Africans do to succeed in this country.

He added that instead of some black men moving around and pimping their sisters, they should be encouraging them to stay in school and get a trade and a job to help raise some of these children in our race. Leroy added that many black men have a bad habit of making many children and leaving them for the black women alone to raise them.

He advised that the black man should learn from the Africans and be a strong family man by copying the Africans' family centeredness to strengthen the black American family structure by being responsible to their women and children and not running away when the first problem occurs in their relationships.

Leroy said, "Many of our young black men think that it is cute to stand at the corner and hustle by selling all kinds of dope, crack, and other drugs to destroy the minds of our sisters and brothers."

Leroy continued to say that such black men should emulate some of these Africans who come here to do all kinds of menial jobs and go through college or trade schools or set up small businesses or drive taxis to save their monies to take care of their families.

Leroy ended by saying that, "our brothers should not continue to hang out on street corners and bullshit and drink cheap liquor. They must begin to see how hard their African brothers work to develop themselves in a land that is foreign to them." Leroy said he has seen many Africans work seven days a week and still go through college to become doctors, engineers, and teachers, while many black men give excuses for their miserable plight in America, and some continue to blame the white man and slavery for their problems. Leroy added that many black Americans who complain about slavery and the white man have the victim mentality and their main problem is that most of them do not have ambition and drive to achieve what they want. Furthermore, Leroy told us that some black American men believe that there is no need to waste all their time to go to school, because the white man will not give them any jobs when they graduate.

He added that black men should learn that going to school does not mean that somebody has to give them jobs, but it means they have honed and developed their brains and acquired more knowledge to embark upon any venture they have in mind—be it business, jobs, teaching.

Leroy continued to say that instead of the black man worrying about the white man's racism and discrimination, or being envious of some of these Africans, he should be concentrating on the ways to develop himself to succeed in America. He added that the black ministers could pave the way for the black masses by investing in apartments, houses, and condominiums at a reasonable price for their memberships and ensuring that they maintain them in decent condition.

He added that more black churches should establish elementary schools, high schools, and colleges, and embark upon exchange student programs with African nations. He said these ventures could later employ the black children who graduated from the schools.

Finally Leroy told us that black churches should make it mandatory to give scholarships each year for at least five youngsters to attend colleges all over Africa, to increase social and academic interactions with Africans in the motherland.

SHIRLEY SPEAKS OUT

A black lady, Shirley who lives in Brooklyn, New York but was raised in downtown New Orleans, told us that she refers to herself as a black American and not as an African American. She said she was raised as a black person in America with a southern Creole background and definitely not an African background.

Shirley told us that when she was in school, all that she learned about Africa was that Africa was a big jungle and rolling grassland with lions and tigers roaming about everywhere on the continent.

She said she saw African women exposing their breasts and the men with small loincloths twisted around their waists and bows and arrows in their hands. She said she did not know that the lions and tigers shown on television were filmed at government-reserved safaris that many white tourists frequented when they visited Africa. She said she was unaware that Africa had cities that have more than a million people with modern buildings, like where she lived at in New Orleans.

She told us that her first impression when she hears about Africa is a place where men are allowed to marry many women and there is a high occurrence of promiscuous lifestyles, which is fueling the AIDS pandemic on the continent.

But she admitted that in some ways she respects the African men, because even though they come from poor countries, they perform all kinds of menial jobs, discipline themselves, go through schools and colleges, and establish themselves well. She said the average African man is a family man who supports his wife and children like white men do. She said a lot of these street black men who are hustling, hanging around street corners, getting high on dope and getting drunk on cheap liquor, and making babies they do not take care of need to learn from these Africans and become responsible fathers for their women and children.

Shirley said the sad part of their problem is that there are many government programs and charitable grants for these black men to go to trade schools and colleges to learn skills to find jobs that are abundant here in America so they can support "their women instead of pimping us and calling us bitches."

Shirley said these street black men who refuse to take advantage of the immense resources, wealth, and abundant opportunities in America to develop themselves often resent the African who comes to America to struggle to succeed.

She added that many Africans make an investment in themselves, whereas these street blacks only complain, talk a lot about nothing, and do not really want anything in life.

She concluded that the African man is not as violent as many black men in America. She said those Africans she has met are mild-mannered compared to the black man in America, who is quick to anger and later regrets what he did, but in most cases does irreparable damage

Shirley said she believed that the African is still inferior to the blacks in America, because she sees the Congolese pygmies running naked with rings in their noses and tribesmen widening their lips with all kinds of plates.

She detests Africans eating with their bare hands like some wild barbarians, and so she thinks they should learn to eat with forks and knives.

When we asked her about her personal experience with an African, she responded that an African graduate from a major university helped her find her current employment.

HARVEY IN NEWARK RESPONDS

Another black American, Harvey, a vice-president of a large Manhattan-based corporation who was raised in Newark, New Jersey, says he refers to himself as African American because that communicates his ancestry.

He said blacks have been called all kinds of names, from "Negro" to "colored" and now "African American." He said when he hears the word *Africa* the dominant theme that comes to his mind is enslavement, because his ancestors were brought from Africa as slaves. He continued to say that the entire continent was subjected to enslavement during the partitioning of Africa by the European nations. Harvey told us that he visited Morocco with an American team to play basketball.

He informed us that not all black Americans categorized Africans as inferior, but even those who have misconceptions about Africa learn them unconsciously from the wicked, deliberated, and perverted propaganda warfare against the African race by its enemies.

He said, "Most of our black guys have made assumptions about the Africans and erroneously claim that Africans are hostile toward black Americans, without getting the chance to meet and interact with the Africans."

He added that a lot of black Americans have allowed this hearsay, or what their friends think and say about Africa, to affect their perceptions and influence their opinion about Africans.

He confessed that he acted as if and believed in his heart that the Africans are arrogant do not respect black Americans, because that was the message going around in his neighborhood, and so that was the assumption of most of his peers. Harvey told us that blacks must learn to say hello to the average African they meet, seek to make genuine friendships with those that are willing to, and test their assumptions about them.

Harvey said he tested his assumptions about Africans by getting to know a man from Ghana named Ali, and he found him to be an excellent friend. And for many years since their youthful days they have continued to be friends. Today Ali is the godfather of his son, who is twenty-five years old. Harvey said that black Americans should learn that "we are all after the same thing, our economic and financial emancipation."

GEORGE FROM OHIO WEIGHS IN

And then we met and spoke with a black man from Cleveland, Ohio. George refers to himself as Afro-Indian American because he is mixed with African, Indian, and European blood with a speck of Chinese blood. He added, "As you can tell, I am a little mixed up, and that is why I often have mixed emotions." He told us that even though the white man erroneously refers to Africa as the Dark Continent, it was still the cradle of mankind.

George added that slavery was common all over the world and not just in Africa. He said the Jews were sold into slavery in Egypt, the Britons were slaves during the Roman Empire, and many Russians and Eastern Europeans were referred to as *Slavs* because they were nothing but slaves in their lands. George added that a lot of Europeans were slaves in America, but they covered their slavery condition with nice and fanciful terms like *indentured servants*. But essentially all these so-called servants were nothing but slaves because they worked freely for their slave masters, who had the authority over them.

He said because these so-called indentured servants were whites, they were able to blend easily into the dominant white society and escape the badge of inferiority that became the lot of the former black slaves.

George informed us that many black Americans look upon Africans as strange and backward because they do not know their customs.

He confessed that most Africans he has met were nice to him and helped him when he needed them. He ended by saying he loved African leaders like Jomo Kenyatta and Nkrumah for fighting against the white man.

THE REACTION FROM MISSISSIPPI

A ninety-year-old black American man, Virgil from Holly Springs, Mississippi, who came to New York City in 1939, said that the greatest black man in history, Nelson Mandela, is an African; therefore, he has a lot of respect for African people for fighting to liberate their people and trying to build their impoverished nations.

He said Mandela endured all kinds of hardships for more than twenty-seven years in jail and still became president without allowing bitterness and hostility to dominate his thoughts. Instead he worked to make South Africa a more peaceful and stable society.

He told us that, apart from all the mere emotional words many black Americans spew about Africans, deep down in their hearts, they love and admire and have a sense of mystery about their African brothers and sisters. He said if we doubted his assertion we should remember how black Americans turned out in hundreds of thousands to meet and greet the great President Nelson Mandela when he came to Harlem.

He added that if black Americans truly did not like or care for the Africans, they would have boycotted en-masse Mandela's visit to Harlem.

Virgil told us that Africans are smart, strong, and resilient people, because look at what the Europeans and Arabs have done to them and their continent: enslaved them, burned down many towns and cities while uprooting the best and most able-bodied people on the continent, colonizing the entire continent again and again. But in spite of all these abuses, the Africans rise and continue to rise to attain their freedom and self respect.

He said Africans are still building their societies in spite of all the relentless negative attacks on them from many Europeans and Asiatic nations. He indicated that black Americans can look down upon the Africans all they want, but the African still has his own country, and "try to raise themselves, whereas the black American does not have his country but lives by the dictates and the whims of the white man, and we continue to this day to obey what our former slave masters order us to do, because if we disobey him he will hurl us into his crowded prisons."

Virgil told us that he has seen all the Tarzan movies but added that only childish, infantile, unthinking people would believe that these childish, perverted myths revealed in these backward movies reflect the actual life in Africa. He said many of these derogatory movies about Africa are the perverted imaginations of Africa's enemies and represent attempts to trick black Americans to look down upon their own kith and kin on the African continent. Virgil admitted that many sophisticated and educated black Americans he had known all throughout his life scoff at these childish and offensive Tarzan movies and do not allow their children to watch them.

He said those blacks who believe in Tarzan nonsense should bow down their heads in shame for allowing the white man to play tricks on their naïve minds.

Virgil said, as the white man is a busy making movie depicting the African as jungle barbarian, he is also showing black Americans as criminals and clowns to the rest of the world. "It's all the traditional divide and conquer." Virgil said many of his friends in Mississippi and New York do not believe in the foolish Tarzan movies and the rest of the negative documentaries against Africa and Africans, because they believe that the white man likes to play a lot of tricks on his television and portray black people in negative terms to brainwash unsuspecting people.

Virgil finally concluded that only childish minds in black America continue to believe the blatant lies about Africa and Tarzan and Jane.

Virgil, however, cautioned Africans to stop their barbaric culture of castrating, or excising, women's clitoris. He said such unwholesome practices deform women and give ammunition for Africa's enemies to use as propaganda capital against the peace-loving Africans.

THE INFAMOUS WILLIE LYNCH'S LETTER

Deborah, a veteran social worker living in New Haven, Connecticut, emphatically asserted that in a pluralistic society like America black Americans are definitely not a monolithic body but are divided by class, caste, education, religion, geographic location, and other groupings.

She said the slave master cleverly classified any baby with even an ounce of black blood as a black American, and therefore there are blacks with Irish, Scottish, English, German, Dutch, French and Spanish bloods.

She said to muddy the waters and further confuse the blacks to insure their total stranglehold on their minds and to prevent unnecessarily slave uprisings, they employed a shrewd technique of divide and conquer advocated by Willie Lynch, a British slave owner. She told us that the so-called Willie Lynch letter served the slave master well, because its methods continue to perpetuate the strong divisions and distrust among black Americans to this day. She said every serious black leader must read the Willie Lynch letter.

As advised, we searched for and found the Willie Lynch letter, written in 1712. Below is the letter in its entirety:

Gentlemen, I greet you here on the banks of the James River in the year of our Lord one thousand seven hundred and twelve. First, I shall thank you, the gentlemen of the Colony of Virginia for bringing me here. I am here to help you solve some of your problems with slaves. Your invitation reached me on my modest plantation in the West Indies where I have experimented with some of the newest and still the oldest methods for control of slaves. Ancient Rome would envy us if implemented. As our boat sailed south on the James River, named for our illustrious King, whose version of the Bible we cherish. I saw enough to know that your problem is not unique. While Rome used cords of wood as crosses for standing human bodies along it's old highway in great numbers, you are here using the tree and the rope on occasion.

I caught the whiff of a dead slave hanging from a tree a couple of miles back. You are not only losing valuable stock by hangings, you are having uprisings, slaves are running away, your crops are sometimes left in the fields too long for maximum profit, you suffer occasional fires, your animals are killed. Gentlemen, you know what your problems are; I do not need to elaborate. I am not here to enumerate your problems; however, I am here to introduce you to methods of solving them.

In my bag here, I have a foolproof method for controlling your black slaves. I guarantee every one of you that if installed correctly, it will control the slaves for at least 300 years. My method is simple. Any member of your family or your overseer can use it.

I have outlined a number of differences among the slaves, and I take these differences and make them bigger. I use fear, distrust, and envy for control purposes. These methods have worked on my modest plantation in the West Indies and it will work throughout the south. Take this simple list of differences, and think about them.

On the top of my list is 'Age' but it is there only because it starts with an "A"; the second is "Color" or Shade, there is Intelligence, Size, Sex, Plantation, Status on Plantation, Attitude of owners, whether the slave live in the valley, on the hill, east, west, north, south, have fine hair, coarse hair, or is tall or short.

Now that you have a list of differences, I shall give you an outline of action- but before that I shall assure you that Distrust is stronger than Trust, and Envy is stronger than Adulation, respect or Admiration.

The black slave after receiving this indoctrination shall carry on and will become self-refueling and self-generating for hundreds of years, maybe thousands.

Don't forget you must pitch the old black male vs. the Young black male and the young black male against the old black male. You must use the dark skin slave vs. the light skin slaves and the light skin slaves vs. the dark skin slaves. You must use the female vs. the male, and the male vs. the female. You must also have your white servants and overseers distrust all blacks, but it is necessary that your slaves trust and depend on us. They must love, respect and trust only us.

Gentlemen, these kits are your keys to control. Use them. Have your wives and children use them, never miss an opportunity. If used intensively for one year, the slaves themselves will remain perpetually distrustful. Thank you, gentlemen. 4

BILLY DENIGRATES TARZAN

Another black American, Billy, a college educated man from the Bronx, New York, told us that he refers to himself as African American because his people, the Africans, are the original people in the world.

He said all world history originated from Africa and that Africa's enemies have tried desperately to destroy the image of the African by making comical jokes about the African for the sole consumption of the black Americans so they have no desire to live in Africa to help the country develop. Billy said every black scholar needs to study African history to understand the history of mankind.

He added that when God said, "Let's make man in our image," and took dust to form man, God was only speaking to the African because dust is not white but either black or brown, indicating the originality of the black race.

He reminded us that even the Europeans unconsciously refer to Africans as aborigines, which means "from the original people created by God," which the rest of mankind evolved from.

Billy said because of the deep-seated fear the white race has of the black race, they go through an inordinate amount of trouble and an exorbitant financial burden to manufacture all kinds of myths like Tarzan movies and other derogatory images to concoct the notion of the inferiority of the black race.

Billy added that those black Americans and Africans who watch and actually believe in the authenticity of Tarzan movies are big fools for believing these myths and lies about themselves and their ancestry.

Billy continued to educate us that Europeans virtually destroyed Africa. During 1884 to 1885, there were mad and reckless scrambles for African lands and wealth.

He said they divided Africa into little countries to weaken its tiny nations and force them to depend upon Europe or risk military attack. And even after independence these African nations are still under the thumbs of these European nations.

Billy revealed that he has spoken to many Africans and none of them claim to be superior or better than the black Americans. If anything at all, most of them are fascinated by black Americans in sports, movies, boxing, and music. He said the average African in America has too many problems with societal adjustments, immigration, and financial hardships to worry about being superior to the black natives of America.

He asked us, "What is the position of Africans in America? - But an inferior status or virtually no status at all. So how can anybody even imagine that these foreigners have a superior attitude toward the blacks born in America?"

Billy concluded that all the Tarzan movies about Africa are corruption and lies on the television that Africans dismiss as mere childish games. And as for cheetah, he would be a good meal for a hungry man in the Congo.

CHARLIE'S PERCEPTION FROM INDIANAPOLIS

Finally we met and spoke with Charlie from Indianapolis, Indiana who told us that he calls himself African American because his ancestors came from Africa. He said Africa is the motherland of all black Americans, but because of the constant attack on Africa and the negative stereotyping of Africans, some black Americans are ashamed to identify themselves with Africa. He cautioned, however, that normal human beings couldn't and must not believe everything they see or hear on television and radio. Most of these negative images of Africa on television are not really true or tell only a small part of the African story.

He further stated that most of the Tarzan movies and other documentaries about Africa are for mere entertainment, and serious and really intelligent brains must never believe such foolishness. He added that anybody who seriously believes that Africans are inferior to black Americans or vice versa should have their brain examined to see if they are actually normal.

He said all human beings are the children of God, even though they progress at different levels. He reminded us that Africans have done damn well considering the immense and relentless attacks on them, the destruction and pillaging of their continent by the white race, and the enslavement of their able-bodied people and over hundreds of years of exploitation and continual attacks on them.

Charlie said, "Today, look at the American Indians. They have been silenced and placed in reservations, and are gradually dying away from the face of the earth; but look at the Africans and how they continue to fight back against their enemies, declare their independence, and slowly but surely build their nations."

He said only dumb people will say that Africans speak funny because they have accents. "Then we can say that French, Dutch, Polish, Spanish, Russians, and Italians speak funny because they all speak English with accents."

Charlie emphasized that almost all Africans speak several languages, including English, and it would be wise if some of our blacks who are laughing at their accents could at least bring themselves to learn only one foreign language to broaden their outlook in the world.

Charlie said many Africans he has met spend a lot of time disciplining themselves to go to school or have a trade to succeed in America. He said when he compares the hardworking Africans in America, to some black Americans, he feels ashamed to see some of the intelligent black men dropping out of school, standing on corners, and selling drugs or loose cigarettes and asking, "What is going on?"

Charlie added that he did not mind blacks collecting government welfare checks, if only they are using the welfare as a stepping stone to better themselves and are not perpetually dependent on them. He explained that such dependency ultimately hurts the blacks because it undermines their ambitions, motivations, drive, and determination to succeed and achieve their dreams or attain their goals in life.

Charlie ended by informing us that most blacks know very little about Africa, and the little they know are all negative images from the television and the assumptions they have accumulated in their heads or what some other poorly informed person has told them.

SIX

ROXANNA, THE COAUTHOR WHO WAS born and raised in Buffalo, New York, has been married to her husband, Kwame, for over twenty-two years. She said that Kwame, like many African men she knows, is a dedicated family man who is devoted to his wive and is supportive of her. She said many African men she knows are very devoted to their marriages and work hard to insure that their marriages are successful.

She said her husband interacts with her sons by teaching them African stories and proverbs and relates those real-life situations to those proverbs and stories to make sure the children are well grounded to face social challenges. She said her husband plays soccer and other games with the children continually, and he is always available to his children, no matter busy he may be.

She added that the success of her marriage is partly dependent on the fact that Kwame is like her best friend who confides some of his most intimate secrets to her. And she also confides in him. She added that this makes it easier for them to discuss the options and actions to be taken in most circumstances, and they both advise each other on critical issues without allowing friends and other family members to interfere or influence their decisions or undermine their friendship.

She said it is difficult for friends and family to undermine their friendship, because they are open with each other, informing each other of what others gossip to them or about each other.

She added that they openly discuss every issue and sometimes haggle over the correct decisions to be made. And desist from playing childish mind games to deceive the other. She added that when an African man sincerely commits to his marriage, he becomes a devoted husband and genuinely respects his wife and treats her as a precious being—instead of so much pretense and "bullshit" she saw growing up in Buffalo.

Roxanna said most Africans believe in education and will move heaven and earth to ensure that their children receive the best education money can buy. She said when she married her husband she was a license practical nurse, but Kwame raved, ranted, and pressured her to continue her education.

She confessed that she was a little apprehensive to enroll in the nursing school of her choice in New York City. She said Kwame escorted her into the director of admissions office and jokingly informed the director that her wife was seeking admission to her college but was afraid to come to her office to apply to the school. Roxanna told us that the admissions director replied, "We do not bite or eat people; here are your application forms." She said Kwame insisted the forms be filled out and submitted to the school there and then, which they did.

She was offered admission and became the vice-president of the student body during her final year. She graduated from the school, passed her registered nursing licensure examination, and is now a full-fledged registered nurse.

She emphasized that Africans are able to network to help each others' families to succeed, because during her nursing school days her husband asked his friend Akuoku to tutor her in chemistry, which he did, and this was tremendously instrumental in her success in school.

Roxanna added that her husband, like many Africans, is deeply spiritual and works from his heart. She said this spirituality about Africans makes them put God first in almost everything they do, and this contributes to the high morality that permeates most things they do, which contributes to making them excellent husbands, especially those who genuinely commit themselves to their marriages.

She admitted that her husband does many things to please and satisfy her, including sharing household chores and working together on almost everything in the house, which makes life easier for her.

Roxanna confessed that there are some problems in marrying an African. She admitted that many of the men are not as physically affectionate as the black American men are. She said many are not physically embracive—touching, frequent hugging, public kissing and caressing, looking deeply into the eyes, and frequently telling their women they love them.

She said some of them can also be controlling and demanding about everything around the house, since they want to be the leader and the boss in their household.

Roxanna finally revealed that many African men feel compelled to provide financial support to their extended family members, most of whom can be as old as Methuselah.

She said an even more worrisome and annoying aspect of marrying an African is the ubiquitous presence of the extended family members, who are often jealous of the American wives. She said some of them sit around and speak in their foreign tongues to conceal their jealousies.

She added that if the husbands are supportive, these problems can easily be smoothed out. She ended by saying that these pesky cultural nuances must be discussed and explained prior to the marriage for both parties to understand and come to some form of agreement.

PERCEPTIONS FROM OUR CHILDREN

Our eldest son, Kwame Jr., who was born in Buffalo, New York, attended Indiana State University and is now a senior at State University of New York. He said he has spoken to many African students and one theme keeps coming up on their perceptions about many black Americans.

He told us that many Africans look at many black Americans and wonder why they do not take advantage of the numerous opportunities available in America to develop themselves and forget about the victim mentality of blaming all their problems on racism and the effects of slavery.

He said many Africans look at the behaviors of many black Americans youths and think they are ignorant, disrespectful, and ill mannered and use plenty of curse words to express themselves. And they think some are violent; therefore, many Africans do not befriend them.

He added that many black Americans also discredit Africans and look down upon them because they were not born in America. They think they come from underdeveloped and backward nations; therefore, they avoid them.

We reminded young Kwame that when Eastern Europeans come from their relatively underdeveloped countries, the white people here in America accept them, work with them, and treat as their brothers and sisters. What prevents the black Americans from doing the same?

Our nineteen-year-old son, Robert Afadzi Insaidoo, who was born in Buffalo, New York, attended Pine Forge academy in Pennsylvania and is now a student of the University of Ghana.

He wrote in a prefatory commentary to his upcoming book that is a fitting conclusion to this section of our work. We have reproduced parts of this work with his full permission. He wrote:

> The sense of community among African Americans has broken down since the righteous 1960s and 1970s. The time is gone when neighbors or friends of family were given the authority to discipline a child who is not their own for the betterment of the community. The entertainment industry is emulated in our communities. Plenty of liquor stores are put in our communities, as opposed to maybe one or two in the omega communities {white communities}. Drugs are much easier for our youth to get access to in our communities.
>
> Public schools are very poorly funded in many alpha communities {black communities}. Therefore this discourages the child slightly and makes him or her want to retreat into the enlarged entertainment industries in our communities.
>
> Not only does the omega race do these things to break down the people in African American communities, but they also focus on breaking down the families directly. Since we kept each other's kids in line within the communities by discipline, something popped up that said that children {minors} have the right to call the police on their parents if they were disciplined 'too hard' for something they genuinely did wrong. It is called "child protective services." A social structure that seems to have been designed to break down highly disciplined families {African American families}, but if entertainment is at its peak in African American communities, parents must subsequently discipline their children more.
>
> Thus it is evident that the child protective services were put into place by the government to break down good African American homes.

The criminal justice system is one social structure that is used in a repulsive way to creatively filter young African Americans out of their communities when they are in their prime. Young African Americans are being targeted with the "crime control method." Crime control means that if you have been in jail before, then you are bad enough to be thrown in jail again. Subsequently the police can pin a lot of small minor crimes on African Americans just to get them into the system. Police use crimes such as traffic violations, petty larceny, fighting in public, or even being too rowdy in a neighborhood party.

Then after African Americans have a record they are targeted even more because of the color of their skin. They are harassed by officers and eventually thrown into jail, primarily because of their so-called past records. Once small crimes pile up, you look like a big troublemaker when you were really just going through the stages of adolescence. For example, I am from Long Island, New York, and I know a jailhouse in Riverhead that houses criminals in both the Nassau and Suffolk county areas. If these two counties are composed mostly of people of European descent, then why is the jailhouse full of African Americans and Latinos?

The police are sworn to protect and serve the community, not to racially profile people. This bad relationship between African American youth and the police goes back to the times of the Black Panther Party. The Black Panther Party was a violent political group that emerged during the peak of oppression of African Americans (the civil rights movement).

The gang that emerged after the Black Panther Party split into two main gangs, much like the great schism in religion. Children join these street gangs because the families of African Americans were and still are being broken down by the system.

The youths seek love in the streets and in any other place they can, among friends when love is not provided to them at home for some reason. Those two main gangs are now called the Crips and the Bloods.

They both at one point in time aimed to do positive things for our African Americans, much like the Panthers did. As things got rougher for African Americans they sort of gave up hope and resorted to illegal means to feed their families. Thus continues the breakdown of African American families.

The omega race (last race) is jealous that they are not alpha (among the first human race).

Alpha males by binomial nomenclature are the first humans to walk this earth. As it was stated in the Holy Bible (Genesis 2:7) that the first men on earth were literally created by God with the clay of the earth, which is brown.

I suggest that all African Americans should come back to Africa. This type of community will sanction you when you do wrong things. This advocates the type of community that we all want for our children and ourselves. America gives our minors an option to separate themselves from family when they are going through rebellious stages and need parents the most.

They can seek emancipation at the tender age of fifteen; not to mention that truant officers will soon be on their backs, allowing the system to once more take control of our youth. This makes it more imperative for all African Americans to come back to Africa.

KORY WEIHGS IN FROM COLLEGE

Our family friend, Kory, born in America, now a junior at an Alabama Technical College, whose father comes from South Africa, reminded us that many black Americans look down on the Africans because of a variety of reasons. He said when the blacks look at the evening news on their television sets, the news coming from Africa is not encouraging, especially the militaristic nature of their governments, where coup d'etats, political instability, civil wars, rebellions, and rampant assassinations are common. He said these political turmoils in Africa reflect negatively on the African people, making many black Americans wonder whether Africans are mature enough to govern themselves.

Kory said, since Africans became independent there has been one political problem after the other, which has prevented African nations from developing their numerous resources. When black Americans look at Africa they wonder what kinds of people continually fight and steal valuable resources from their own countries to impoverish them.

He said many black Americans look down upon the native Africans because they are desperately poor with an inadequate and underdeveloped infrastructure. He said black Americans think Africans lack good roads, electricity, efficient sanitation, and in most cases they do not have an existing healthcare system and diseases wreak havoc on the population. Kory added that what irritates most black Americans is that the African politicians, statesmen, and scholars (after destroying their nations with their incompetence and kleptomaniac behavior) ran away from their nations to America and want to thumb their noses at the blacks in America.

He said many blacks are asking that if Africans are that good, why they are running away from their continent? Why don't they stay at home to help build their African continent? Why are they coming to America with a song and a dance to seek political or economic asylum?

Kory said additionally that Africans come from a society that emphasizes the importance of education. He said most Africans believe that formal schooling is the road to economic and financial security, and so education to them is paramount, and most of them spend inordinate amount of years in schools educating themselves and their children; and they wonder why many blacks in America do not do likewise.

He said the Africans do not understand why many blacks do not view the significance of education, its numerous benefits, and how it can help them overcome some of their financial problems.

Kory said what the Africans do not understand is that most blacks do not see education as the only road to financial prosperity. He said the blacks live in America, where there are numerous opportunities open to them. He said some black Americans make millions of dollars playing basketball, football, and baseball. He said some make hundreds of millions of dollars singing songs. Blacks are emerging hip hop artists. Boxers, movie stars, and other entertainers make millions of dollars, while some college graduates with doctorates cannot find reasonable jobs to make a decent living.

We agree with Kory that all kinds of opportunities to make millions of dollars exist in America, but for every black person who is lucky enough to be drafted into NBA basketball, there are numerous black people whose dreams did not materialize.

We challenged him that the same statistics hold true in other areas, like music, acting, entertainment, boxing, and other avenues. While the few lucky and talented ones are able to achieve stardom, there are countless others shoved by the wayside. Our solution, therefore, to any aspiring black actor, basketball player, athlete, or musician is to attend formal schooling to college completion and then veer off to their bliss or their calling. That way they have their education to fall back on in addition to their dreams and goals, in case those dreams do not come true.

SEVEN

THE AFRICAN RESPONSE

We turned our attention to the Africans who have lived in America for more than a decade and have had many interactions with the black Americans to determine their opinions and reactions toward the treatment they have received or continue to receive from the blacks.

We wanted to investigate how the blacks treat the Africans in America. Are the blacks nice to them? Do they treat the Africans with hostility? Are they accepting of the Africans, and what do the Africans do to the blacks to receive whatever treatment or reaction they get from the blacks? Are the Africans arrogant to the blacks, as many blacks claim them to be? Are the Africans fearful of the blacks because of incessant television propaganda that claims that blacks are prone to crime and are to be feared? Do the Africans assume that black Americans will instinctively understand them when they speak, even though some of them speak English with accents that are often difficult for the average American to understand?

The first African response to the many hydra-headed problems emerging from several sources was a Gambian Harvard graduate, Seidu, who inspired us with many of his discussions about the black American.

Seidu informed us that he empathizes with black Americans' plight in America, because they were forcibly uprooted from their traditional African societal milieu and brought to an alien land for the expressed purpose of economic exploitation, during which they endured all kinds of unimaginable and horrendous inhuman abuses.

He said black Americans continue to suffer through no fault of their own, and of course they have the right to be upset and angry about the way they are being treated and their general condition in America. He said black Americans can't afford to continue to endure oppression in America and have a duty to their grandchildren to do something about their plight in America. He said it's all right few blacks are elevated to national prominence, but for black Americans to gain political power, use their huge economic leverage in the emerging globalization, and remove their current societal marginalization in America, blacks have to adopt two important states in the union. He said the Jewish people overwhelmingly settled in New York City, and now have tremendous political and economic power in New York, which has national ramifications, so much so that our beloved Rev. Jesse Jackson once referred to New York City as "hymie town."

Similarly, Seidu advises that blacks migrate to only two states, like North and South Carolina or any two states of their leaders' choice in America, and consciously and deliberate migrate to just those two states.

He said the current population of black America is now over 35 million, and if these 35 million blacks migrate to only two states, they will literally dominate and become the majority of the population in those two states. He said judging from the trend of white behavior, whenever blacks overwhelmingly move to a new place; there is a white flight, much like what became of most inner cities in America today. He said once the blacks become a majority in both states, that represents huge political and economic power for black Americans. Seidu outlined the immensity of the political and economic power that a movement or migration will provide to black Americans:

- The two adopted states will be overwhelmingly black Americans, because if the entire 35 million blacks migrate into only two states and some whites leave those states, black people will be the predominant race in those two states.

- These will have a major political impact upon all three branches of governments in those states. For one thing, black Americans will occupy the executive powers, and the governors' mansions in both states, and then the states bureaucratic apparatus will be steered mainly by black people because most of the state workers will mainly be blacks. The sweet-deal government contracts that are often awarded to friends will go primarily to black people, which will help solve many of the chronic unemployment problems that confront black Americans on daily basis.

- The state legislative power and indeed the state assemblies will overwhelmingly be occupied by black Americans, and then they can begin the arduous process of creating legal statutes that will take into consideration their effect upon and benefit to the average black American. And of course these lawmakers in these states will debate the necessity of finally abolishing the Ku Klux Klan and all white supremacists organizations from those two states and making any form of racial discrimination a criminal act.

- The judicial systems in both states will be comprised of overwhelmingly black people. Black lawyers will seriously campaign in all parts of both states to be elected to the district attorneys' offices to insure a fair trial for our oppressed people. Judges in both states will be mainly black lawyers who have the interest of their people at heart and hopefully will adjudicate cases that will be fair to all parties concerned, without racial bias or being quick to railroad any person into jail.

- The towns and cities in both states will have mainly black mayors who will administer these cities in the interest of black people.

- The greater impact on the national political level will be the election of four black senators into the United States Senate—two from each state. This will have far-reaching implications of political power for all black Americans living in both states. Moreover, the presidential candidates will not be able to take black Americans for granted anymore because of their need for Electoral College votes from both states occupied by black Americans. Hence, blacks can gain a lot of multiple concessions from these presidential candidates, which will improve the lives of black Americans, whose ancestors have worked and died to build America into what its today in all its grandeur and technological, military, and economic superiority over the entire universe. The United States's material prosperity is unparallel in the annals of history.

- These two states can have strong economic, political, educational, and cultural ties with all black nations, from the Caribbean to the entire African continent and can have trade and other relations that will positively impact both societies.
- The overall economic impact, coupled with its multiplier effect on the entire two states, will be tremendous.

Seidu added that for black Americans to get over their current malaise of their children being thrown into jails for frivolous and minor incidences, and to steer these children into the mainstream society for them to correctly use their undeveloped intelligence, every black child, particularly the boys, should be made to begin the first grade in an African country.

He said these children should be made to finish their primary education in Africa and then transfer their grades to the middle schools here in America. Seidu said this arrangement would have an extremely positive impact on the participating children.

- These children will be attending predominantly black schools with black headmasters and headmistresses, all-black teachers, and all-black administrators who have a stake in the success of these black children. These black teachers understand through their many years of experience how children behave and interact with each other and are less likely to label them with all kinds of unproductive adjectives and throw them into special education classes or label them as troublemakers, which negatively impacts their behaviors. Sometimes when these teachers label these impressionistic black children as unintelligent and unable to learn, unconsciously some of these children take this to heart and believe what these so-called educated teachers tell them, and so they are more likely to drop out of the school system altogether. Sometimes some of these teachers in white schools have low expectations of the black children, or some even come to their classes mirroring the greater society's racist and prejudicial perceptions of black people and transfer those negativities to the young black children in their classes and act in unloving ways, which the growing black children sense in the class, and this makes them uncomfortable in school. But sending these children to African schools removes all these negativities and impediments impacting the black children and places the children in a psychologically healthy atmosphere to enable the child to concentrate on his education. It is healthy because the child is placed in predominantly black societies that have a stake in nurturing black children to become productive citizens of their society. The society does not discriminate against them because of the color of their skin.

- Seidu said when these children return to America to attend the middle schools; they will be prepared psychologically to deal with this system. Those children will have received a cultural training, learned some of the African language, and will know a lot of African history. They will have discovered that their ancestors did not come from the jungle but live in cities, some of which have populations of more than two million people. These children will have a healthy dose of African traditional values, moral values and family morality ingrained in them.

- He said all parents interested in considering sending their children to African schools should go on the Web sites of African countries or call the consular offices of African nations to get the requisite information about schools in African nations. Or better yet they should e-mail their entire request about schooling in Africa to the authors at KInsaidoo@aol.com.

A RESPONSE FROM NIGERIA

Do you remember the Nigerian brother Khalid from Kano in Nigeria? Well, we revisited Khalid, who has been in America now for more than thirty-five years and has obtained his graduate degree from a major university in New York State. Khalid informed us that black Americans are like any human beings on earth; "you have to respect them, and they in turn will respect you." He added, "If you treat people nicely they will also treat you nicely, and if you are nasty and arrogant to them, they will also do likewise."

He told us that in his more than thirty-year stay in America he found out that most black Americans have different cultural perceptions of Africa. For example, some Africans like to eat with their fingers because that is the way they were raised, but some blacks view this practice as unhygienic, barbaric, and primitive.

He told us that he chews chicken bones because the marrow in the bones helps strengthen his teeth, so much so that his teeth are in excellent condition, but most of his black friends laugh at him. He responds to them by saying that his way of eating is just different from theirs but it does not make it barbaric; it makes it just different, because every culture has its modes of behavior and one is not necessarily superior to the other. It is just different.

Khalid said Africans have the responsibility to explain their cultural heritage to the black American who is interested in learning about the various African traditions on the continent. He cautioned the Africans not to easily get upset if the blacks laugh at their cultural practices. These practices may be alien to them because they are born into a society with norms and values that are different from the African. He said the African who travels to America should be more tolerant of the black Americans because of the lies and myths they have been told about Africa.

When we inquired why Africans, particularly Nigerians, call black Americans akata, he responded by telling us that some Africans use the word loosely to refer to all black Americans, but it does not refer to all of them. He educated us that in his estimation, the word *akata* refers to the young black women who are unstable and unreliable. Essentially he defined *akata* as a young woman who smokes profusely, drinks hard liquor, uses all kinds of drugs, and follows all kinds of men indiscriminately. He said such a woman has little respect for herself and her life is not stable because she may not have steady employment and continually follows criminals in the streets.

He told us that this akata behavior is common in the large metropolitan centers, where it's common to find some of these unreliable and unstable women drinking, smoking, drugging, and chasing after gangsters. He reminded us that in small rural towns or states you seldom find or see these akata behaviors; and even in the big cities this behavior is confined to a small group of fast young women.

He related a typical example of what an akata woman did to him. He told us that one day he took a young beautiful black woman into in his apartment after they visited the local mall. He told her to make herself comfortable while he went to the nearest store to buy her soda and other snacks to entertain her. He said when he returned from the store the young woman has stolen his Polaroid camera and his Panasonic radio and had left the house and could not be found anywhere. He said this was typical akata behavior in action. We reminded Khalid that it was dangerous to take strangers into his apartment and he could not blame those strangers or call them some akata names for robbing him, because it was unwise for him to pick up stray women from the streets. We also reminded him that his definition of *akata* fits so many white girls in America, Europe, and many girls in West Africa, Latin America, and Eastern European nations—not just the black American. Hence, Africans must be informed to desist from loosely referring to black Americans as akata.

Khalid also informed us that Africans must understand that black Americans are struggling to attain success in a difficult and racist society like America, and Africans must understand them.

Furthermore, he advised that Africans who have had bad encounters with some blacks must not generalize that all of them do not like the African.

He added that in every society you find people that like you, and those who do not like you; because that is the way the world works.

Khalid cautioned Africans who come to America not to believe everything they see on the television about black people, because most of the shows are propaganda against the black American—the same way negative and demeaning propaganda is shown about Africa's primitiveness.

He advised Africans that the subtle propaganda against black Americans takes several forms, like magnifying small crimes committed by blacks and showing them on the first page of a newspaper, as opposed to a huge crime by whites getting little play and being hidden in the middle obscure page of the same newspaper.

He said black Americans have some of the best and most powerful churches in America and are more spiritual and God-fearing than the whites. He added that Africans must also know that blacks have all kinds of business enterprises, and most of them are employed and earn high salaries; and the combined total earnings of black Americans far exceeds the gross domestic production of any African country, except perhaps South Africa.

Khalid admitted that even though the dominant white society has institutionalized the oppression and discrimination of black Americans, a great deal of them is determined to be free from their bondage and oppression.

He added that he has been in American for over the thirty years and has worked with black Americans in several capacities, and a lot of them are extremely hardworking, if given the chance to prove themselves.

He said the dominant society impresses upon the incoming Africans that the blacks are lazy and that is the reason why they are on welfare rolls, but he said that is only part of the story. He told us that Africans should be careful when looking at the condition of the blacks, because of the inherent racism in America society.

He said in most cases necessity, hopelessness, and extreme suffering make the black person dependent on the welfare system.

Khalid added that Africans should not be brainwashed to believe that there is a high dropout rate among black people going to college.

He said the so-called high drop-out rate is only part of the story, but the rest of the story is that black America has many traditional black colleges that have enrolled and continue to enroll many intelligent, ambitious, and highly motivated black men and women; some of whom are earning advanced degrees in all academic disciplines, including many medical, legal, and pharmaceutical degrees on yearly basis.

He admitted that there may be a drop-out rate, but the white media blows these drop-outs of proportion. Khalid repeatedly informed us that Africans must educate themselves to know the real statistical information of the black American success rate after the civil rights movement.

He said there are many elected black officials from the local, state, and federal levels of government, and there are many blacks in American diplomatic corps spread all over the globe, and Africans must make better inroads to have serious interactions with most of these successful blacks and stop believing in the stereotypes paraded in the media today about the blacks. He emphasized that Africans must not erroneously assume that the blacks in the streets they see and interact with constitute all there is to black America. He said these street blacks represent only the tip of the iceberg of black people in America. There is indeed an inordinate amount of highly successful blacks in American, including many millionaires who are not shown on television for the world to see readily like their white counterparts.

We asked Khalid if he had been married before to a black American, to which he answered that he was married to a black American for more than ten years but it ended in a divorce.

We were curious to know the reasons for their divorce, at least from his perspective, knowing full well that in every divorce there are the men and women's stories and the real truth lies somewhere in between their dramas; but we were curious to hear his side of the divorce drama.

Khalid informed us that his wife did not want him to attend his weekly Nigerian tribal association meetings, and more annoying to her was that whenever he came home he had already eaten dinner at their meetings. He said she was suspicious that he was using those association meetings to meet his Nigerian girlfriend.

He also insisted that as president of the association, he had to attend those meetings, and this became a source of confusion and conflict between them. He also said the tribal association collected dues for the upkeep of their group and to assist members during emergency situations. He said his wife was adamantly opposed to his payment of dues to the association without obtaining prior permission from her, and this became a constant source of conflict.

We agreed with Khalid that it was admirable that he belonged to his tribal association, but to prevent conflicts he should have had a long discussion with his wife prior to their marriage about these associations and let her understand what was involved in these associations, including the required dues.

We further told Khalid that he could have obtained the consent of the association to make his wife an honorary member so that she could have attended all meetings with him, and a source of irritation in the marriage would have been resolved.

Khalid further informed us that another source of conflict in the marriage was that as a Nigerian he was obligated to help support his aging mother by remitting small monthly stipends to her. But his wife objected that he was wasting their family funds on his old African mother. Once again, we responded to Khalid that such important financial arrangements should be discussed long before the ringing of the wedding bells.

It is instructive for all black American women contemplating marrying African men to have an honest discussing about the issue of sending monies to support their aging parents in Africa, because this is a common practice among many successful African men. It is a common practice because many African women go through incredible pain and sacrifice to invest huge amount of their livelihood to educate their sons, hoping that these boys will become successful enough to help take care of them in their old age. This is so because many African nations do not have social security or other governmental benefits for women who did not work in the formal government sector or in a reputable business organization. And today most African men, either out of obligation or altruism, willingly remit money to their aging mothers. This is a good practice because most sensible and wise women know that the way a man treats his mother is how he is likely to treat his own wife.

Let us repeat that all African men contemplating marrying black American and other foreign women have the duty and an important obligation to explain and stress the important of this cultural necessity to their future brides.

On another issue, Khalid told us that many Africans wonder why there is a high concentration of black Americans in jail all over the country. He said some of them make mistakes when they are young, like all other people, and become first offenders, and some of them later become repeat offenders, but generally the criminal justice system in America is skewed or biased against the black American.

He said the overwhelming majority of law enforcement officials are white: most judges, police officers, sheriffs, marshals, district attorneys, and court officials are overwhelmingly white.

Khalid said when a black person is accused of a crime he needs to have good legal representation to seriously and vigorously defend and exonerate himself from the claws of the justice system, but in most cases, because of the pervasive poverty, most blacks cannot afford the exorbitant fees of these high-priced but efficient and effective defense lawyers.

The black man is invariably forced to scrape the bottom of the legal barrel and is forced to be represented by the so-called public defenders, who are paid by the very criminal justice system that is prosecuting the accused black man.

Khalid continued to say that when you coupled this problem with the obvious entrenched and pervasive institutional racism that is endemic in the society, the black person does not stand a chance in this skewed criminal justice system. He said that in most cases the blacks, knowing the overwhelming odds against them, simply agree to plea bargain their cases to get lower jail terms; hence, the growing number of black men and recently black women in American jails.

Khalid spoke to us about the so-called drug epidemic in the black neighborhoods of America. He said the blacks do not control the borders of the nation; they do not own airplanes or fleets of ships to transport these drugs from abroad to black neighborhoods. And yet there is a glut of all kinds of drugs in the black neighborhoods. He challenged us to think of the following critical questions: If the blacks are not bringing these drugs from abroad to their neighborhoods, then who are responsible for bringing all kinds of drugs to their doorsteps? Who spends hundreds of millions of dollars to saturate black neighborhoods with drugs? What is the true purpose of saturating the black neighborhoods with these poisonous drugs? And why is such an expensive drug like cocaine cut cheaply into crack cocaine for only three dollars per vile? Why is alcohol, especially hard liquor, sold inexpensively in black neighborhoods? Is there a hidden agenda to flood black neighborhoods with poisonous drugs and cheap liquor to make them easily accessible to little black boys and girls? Is it to lure them to destroy themselves? Do you all remember the lessons of the Chinese Opium wars, and are there any parallels here?

OMARI'S HORRIBLE EXPERIENCE

Do you recall that in the prefatory commentary, Omari from Cape Coast in Ghana was enthusiastic about meeting black Americans when he traveled to London? He was so proud to see blacks in military uniform that he practically saluted them whenever he saw them, believing them to be super human beings who could help finance Africans to go to school in America.

Well, Omari has lived in New York for forty years and has interacted with black Americans from all walks of life in New York.

His observations of black American interactions with Africans is that generally all blacks, without exception, look down upon the African, and he believes that black Americans deeply believe in their heart of hearts that Africans are inferior to them.

He said that after working, living, going to school, playing, and dating black Americans, he had come to the firm conclusion that these blacks believe unequivocally in their superiority over the African. He added that even the black American women who marry Africans still secretly believe in their hearts that they have lowered themselves a little to be with the backward African, because their often condescending attitudes betray their lies. He challenged Africans married to black Americans to observe how they are treated and compare that with the behavior of their wives around black American men.

Omari said when black Americans hear the Africans speak with their accents; right away they assume their superior posture and attitude toward them and laugh at their so-called funny accents.

He said most black Americans begin their superior attitude toward the African by assuming that since they were born and bred in an advanced country, they are invariably better human beings than the African, who is from an underdeveloped society.

He added that beginning with this false premise, they begin to frown upon anything that the African does and erroneously and naively assume that whatever the African does or even proposes, the black American can do or propose it better. He lamented bitterly that even the most illiterate and backward black American instantly believes that he or she is superior to the most sophisticated Harvard graduate African because he talks funny with an accent.

Omari said during the years of living in New York City, he found out that black Americans are mean-spirited and disagreeable to the African and absolutely do not like the Africans.

He warned all Africans to stay away from these blacks, because ninty percent of them are not only hostile to the Africans, but are troublemakers who will not hesitate to physically harm the African when they cross them the wrong way. He said most of them talk as if they speak from their stomachs and not from their heads.

He advised Africans to be extremely careful around these blacks and not to kid or play around with them because, "You cannot kid around with them, because they take everything very seriously, and when they tell you they will kill you, you better believe it, because they are meanspirited and violent people."

We asked Omari if he will ever consent to work for a black American. He replied that he would never; ever work for a black American in his life again. He said he once worked for a black company and they were very bad and nasty people to work for, because apart from the poor working conditions and the meager wages, they were almost reluctant to pay him. When the payday slowly came around they joked that an African can work for free because he does not need a lot of money to live since he comes from a backward society. He said his black bosses were ill-mannered and treated him in a derogatory manner, as if he was subhuman.

Omari said even if you gave him a million dollars as a gift, he would never consent to marrying a black American woman, because of their unpredictable and mean-spirited behavior. He revealed to us that he once lived with a black woman for two years and it was the most horrible experience in his entire life. He said for one thing, he could never enjoy himself and openly play jovially with her, because she took little petty things seriously and instead of explaining herself and telling him what annoyed her, she chose to scream, rave, and yell like a lunatic.

He said there is absolutely no joy or happiness in marrying and living with these black women and said that is why many successful African college graduates prefer to either marry white women or their native Africans. He added that most of these black women do not seem to know what they really want in a relationship and that everything is a fight with them. Omari demonstrated to us the behavior and head movements of the angry black woman he lived with by shaking his head, waving his fingers, and twisting or moving his waist and walking away. He said she stayed angry all the time. He said the black woman he lived with believed that screaming was a substitute for talking or calmingly explaining herself, and he said that most black women are emotionally unstable.

He revealed that if he were paid a million dollars to marry a black American woman, he would never marry her, because she would aggravate him to an untimely death and the million dollars would still be around. He said most black women have attitudes and like to argue about everything because they naively believe that they know everything and cannot be wrong.

He added that all the Africans he knows who are married to black women have developed high blood pressure because of the aggravation they endure at the hands of their wives.

He said most black people are difficult and strange people, and anytime they open their mouths there is a problem because they act like they know too much of everything, but in actuality most simply are big show-offs or know-it-alls. He said whenever he was training blacks on the job, as soon as you begin to show them something, they burst out saying, "I know that," but when you leave them to do it they fail to get it right.

Omari further informed us that he has spoken to and interacted with hundreds of black Americans in the forty years he has lived in America, and almost all of them deeply believed that Africans sold them into slavery for them to catch hell in American under the slave master; hence, their hostile attitude toward Africans.

He added that most also erroneously believe that the white man brought these incoming African students to the United States with their tax dollars, offered them all kinds of jobs, and made their lives better than the blacks'; this perception of the blacks also fuels their dislike or unfriendliness toward Africans.

Omari said most of them are in jails because schooling is not important to most of them because most believe they will not get jobs after graduating from schools and colleges. But even though most do not finish school or learning a trade, they love the materialism advertised on the television: the latest flashy cars, the best clothes, and all the nice things this capitalistic society has to offer. Hence, some steal, sell drugs, or sell their bodies to buy these modern amenities.

He told us that a lot of them get high on drugs because they believe erroneously that their problems (their financial and societal headaches) will go away because of the temporary euphoric moments that the drugs make them experience. He said many of these street black hustlers peddle these drugs to get money to purchase flashy cars with expensive hubcaps and loud music that gives them away to the police, who often harass them with the least provocation and in some cases confiscate these cars.

He added that many other ethnic groups that sell drugs convert the proceeds from cash into durable wealth-producing assets or use the cash to procure industries, auto mechanic shops, painting business, plumbing businesses, real estate, grocery stores, electrical repair businesses, and other small-scale businesses and leave the drug trade; but some of these black Americans use the drug proceeds lavishly or ostentatiously on flashy cars and high-class women.

He ended by telling us that the black American family structure will continue to be dysfunctional until the overly assertive black women actually begin to believe in God and practice their Christian religion, and not just go to church on Sundays to show off their clothes, hairdos, and latest cars; scream to praise the Lord and then come home to become a devil and raise hell with their husbands.

He added some of these black women have to believe and practice their Christianity unconditionally, and make it really positive in their lives by adhering to God's words in the Bible.

He added that these women should read and practice what their Bible instructs regarding the responsibilities and the duties of a wife, particularly as explained in Ephesians 5:22-24, which reads, "Wives submit to your husbands, as to the Lord. For the husband is the head of the wife, as also Christ is the head of the church; therefore, just as the church is subject to Christ, so let the wives be to their own husbands in everything?"

We also informed Omari that marriage is a two-way process, a friendship, a give-and-a take relationship; it is not a dictatorship of the man. He has to be a responsible person to his wife and children, and provide for them.

We reminded him that black men should not smother, boss around, and abuse their wives in the name of being the leader of their households, but they should learn to communicate effectively and each should respect the other.

Omari said he has finished dealing with black Americans because he had many of them as friends and used to do them favors by taking them home cooking on the weekends and leasing his rooms to some of them at far below the fair market value of housing in New York City.

He revealed that when they saw his television, radios, watches, VCR, computers, printers, and other fancy items in his apartment, they planned to rob him. He told us that they are very ingenious when it comes to doing wrong things like robbery, because they set him up by using his own friend as a diversion, taking him to a nice restaurant to eat and dance with so-called girl friends while others ransacked his apartment and stole everything he had. He said he was robbed like this for more than five times by these so-called black American friends, until an old black lady gave him a tip and told him to stay away from those so-called friends he had, because they were the same friends that had come back in his absence to rob him.

As much as we sympathized and felt sorry for him, we told him that as a foreigner it was unwise to begin associating with people he barely knew in a new society, calling them his friends, and making the critical mistake of taking them to his apartment, thereby exposing himself and his few material possessions to people he barely knew.

We reminded him that, though it was wrong that they robbed him, they did so not because he was an African but because they were bad people who took advantage of his naivety and vulnerability and could have robbed any American, as they usually do.

Omari also revealed that on a different occasion he went out to buy Chinese food, and unbeknownst to him, he was being shadowed by four black American men who saw his wallet when he was paying for his food. He said that on his way home these black deviants accosted him, pushed him down, dislocated his shoulder from its socket, and pointed a loaded gun at him, demanding his money. He said he begged for his life and gave all the money to them, until they let him go. He had worked for two incredible weeks for that money.

On another occasion he said he was dressed up in a suit and was going to work all night at a hotel as a desk clerk, and as he walked past three black American men, one of them knocked him over, attempting to rob him of his Seiko watch and wallet. He said he got up, ran, and galloped like a hare to the nearest police precinct, with cuts and bruises all over his face and legs. He said he could not work that night and had to move from the neighborhood.

Omari lamented that when these same mean-spirited black Americans go to Africa, they expect the Africans to lay the red carpet and welcome them home. He said he is telling his people back home in Africa the poor and hostile way these black Americans treat Africans in America and letting these Africans know to be careful of them.

He added that he would vigorously campaign against any African government that advocates extending dual citizenships to these mean-spirited and terrible people.

We told Omari that as painful as his ordeal was and as much as we felt for him, he should desist being hostile toward all black Americans, because the boys who pulled the gun on him and robbed him and those that chased him for his watch were societal deviants, hoodlums, and vagabonds who also attack black American men, women, and white people, or anybody they can rob.

We reminded him that they did not rob him because he was an African, but they saw an opportunity to attack and rob a victim. They thought they could get away with his money. We told him that these attacks and robberies, as despicable as they were, occurring all over the world, including in his own city of Cape Coast in Ghana, and he has to be extra careful and vigilant to protect himself from these occurrences.

Kwame also related to Omari the ordeal his black American female friend underwent right after her medical school residency in St. Louis, Missouri. He related that the young lady, Rose, who lived alone in her house, was attacked by three big black American men who attempted to rape her, but they stole all her jewelry, money, and all kinds of priceless artifacts. Kwame asked Omari whether Rose should hate all black American men; obviously not, but she should be extra careful about strangers and seek protection for her home by installing burglar alarms, window and door guards, fierce dogs, and may be procure a handgun for her protection.

EMOTIONAL RESPONSE FROM A GHANAIAN LADY

Another Ghanaian nurse we spoke to, Julie complained bitterly that many black Americans do not respect Africans at all, because of their dominant belief that Africans sold them into slavery to suffer in America. Julie said many blacks are simply not nice to Africans, because they treat them badly. She added that in her job as a nursing assistant, she prefers to take care of white patients instead of the black ones, because the whites treat her with respect, make her feel welcome, and know how to relate to her as a human being.

She told us that the white patients trust them. She said they "offer us food and other nice treats, and are generally thoughtful and appreciative of the services provided to them." She said the white patients are so nice to them; they go an extra mile to insure that whatever they require to make their lives a little comfortable is provided to them.

Furthermore, she added that white patients are generally polite and pleasant to work with and are therefore a joy to take care of. She said many of her colleagues fight to get white patients.

She contrasted this pleasant attitude of the white patients with black American patients she had already served. She revealed that when many black Americans hear her accent and conclude that she is an African, they begin to "talk to me like I am a piece of dirt, and they are actually nasty and they scream and bark commands at me, like I am their long-lost slave."

She added that the black patients are "always suspiciously checking on us to see what we are doing, and to say the least, most of them are unappreciative and downright mean-spirited." She continued, "Whenever you do something they do not like, they rub it in your face that I should be glad I am in America and away from the disease, hunger, and filth in Africa."

Julie said after working with the blacks American patients for the last seven years, she has come to the conclusion that "these black Americans believe in their heart of hearts that they are better than us Africans because they live in American and we come from Africa."

Julie concluded by saying that many blacks think that the African still lives in trees today, like the senseless Tarzan movies that are still clouding their intelligence. She asks, "If it weren't for these dumb and childish movies about Africa, why else would an intelligent human being living in the most technologically and scientifically advanced nation like America ask me where I learned English, and speak with less grammatical mistakes like they do, and whether we wear nice clothes like they do here?"

AN IBO MAN SPEAKS OUT

Clement, a Nigerian from the Ibo tribe who has lived in America for over the past ten years, told us that after working with many black Americans his impression about most of them is that some of them are inpatient and allow minor things to quickly drive them to anger, become furious, and often threaten people with violence.

He added that it is as if most of them refuse to calmly and patiently face challenges and slowly use their heads to unemotionally resolve their problems.

Clement said he has worked with many nice, educated black Americans, but his main problem with them is that they are generally quick to anger, as if they are the only ones with tempers.

Clement told us that the word *akata,* used to describe black Americans by Nigerians, is not an abusive word; neither is it an insult. He said it is used to denote the fact that blacks have their own cultural mode of behavior, which is entirely different from the African, who sometimes views their behavior as peculiar compared to their own, which is to be expected because they have different societal values, norms, and cultural beliefs.

Clement told us that many of these black youngsters are languishing in jails in large numbers. He believes this is because they hang out in the streets and allow peer pressure to influence them to pick up street behavior, which includes a lack of respect for themselves and authority figures.

He said these youngsters' disrespect for their elders and parents later develops to the disrespect of societal laws and disobeying those who are charged with enforcing these laws by calling them names like "pigs." He said that this disrespect for societal laws leads many of these youngsters straight into the jailhouses.

He added that proper education, strict parental guidance, and the influence of the churches help many of these young black boys and girls begin to respect themselves and authority figures, which is crucial in nurturing the much needed self-esteem of these youngsters to save them from the clutches of the criminal justice system.

Clement also noted that many black children do not have patience, passion, dedication, and the much needed discipline to complete the tedious academic process, because of the instant gratification and get-rich-quick schemes advertised in the popular media. "As a result," he said, "many of the most intelligent and brilliant black boys end up in the street selling drugs, and most end up either dead or in jail."

THEN THE YORUBA RESPONDS

Another Nigerian, Oga from the Yoruba tribe who has lived in America for the past forty-two years, said many black Americans are quick to categorize and dismiss anything African as inferior or bad without giving themselves ample time and opportunity to experience whatever it is they are looking at or being asked to do.

Oga continued that once the African perceives that the black American looks condescendingly at him, he begins to be suspicious of his motives and moves and learns to stay away from them.

He said this attitude and sour atmosphere bring about the separation between them, with each side looking suspiciously at the other.

A VIEW FROM CONAKRY

Then we encountered Laye from Conakry, Guinea, who has worked in America as automobile body mechanic for the past twenty years. He complained bitterly about the hostile behavior of many black Americans.

He said as a body mechanic he works on people's cars, repairing damage and painting cars for his customers, and he has received several commendations about his meticulous and high quality of work from his many customers.

He told us that recently he noted a trend among several of his black American male customers that has made him reluctant to work on their cars, because of the games they are playing with him.

He revealed that when the black men come to his shop and hear his African accent, they begin to play their vicious games with him. He said they play this game by giving him their cars to work on. Then they inspect the finished work, pay their money, and take their cars home.

He said after five days, these same guys would return in groups of four to claim that the work was not well done and demands their money back in full, or else they threaten to "fuck" him and his business up.

He told us that since he works in a shop in the bad part of town, he is afraid that if he does not refund their money, they will beat him up, burn his shop or do something bad to him. He added that nowadays he is hesitant to accept work from black American men.

THE TANZANIAN REACTION

Makuma, a Tanzanian doctoral candidate in media ecology expressed shock and disbelief that nearly a whole race of black Americans could allow themselves to be manipulated by the power of the media.

He said Hollywood— using powerful, cutting-edge, revolutionary movie methods; tricky visual and special effects; and great performances with good actors—has been successful in brainwashing most black Americans to believe that African society is like the Tarzan movies.

He added that Hollywood has been playing with the minds of black Americans by sometimes using computer-generated images or simulations of nature by cutting and pasting and superimposing these so-called African jungles on the television screens as virtual realities of life in Africa.

He laughed that these special effect movies of Tarzan and other derogatory movies that depict the so-called uncivilized Africans living in jungles, saying they are not the real life in the African society and should not be believed.

He said the movie *Superman* is another tricky device of Hollywood using simulations, computer-generated visual effects, and great acting to convince undeveloped and infantile minds that a mere mortal can have abnormal powers to fly to the skies, mountains, and buildings and land safely back on earth.

Makuma said anytime he speaks to the black Americans and they laugh at his accent and the fact that he came from Africa, he cannot help but feel sorry for them for allowing themselves to be fooled and made ignorant of Africa by the media propaganda. He lamented bitterly and asked, "Don't these blacks know that there are many white people in Africa who are fighting in Southern Africa and Zimbabwe to stay in Africa?"

THE DANCER FROM GUINEA

The story of Fanta from Conakry, Guinea is interesting to note. This is the young lady whose great grandparents told her about how Arabs had kidnapped some of her forebears and sold them to the slave dealers, who took them away to America.

She told us that she was excited to come to America to meet the descendants of her people, her long-lost brothers and sisters. She said she has been in America for the past fifteen years and that many of the black Americans treat her like she is a piece of garbage.

In her limited English, she complained bitterly that, "They treat me like I am nothing. They treat me and my African friends very bad, like we are not human beings, or like we are stupid and dumb." She said as a home attendant, when the black Americans hear her African accent, they do not want her to sit on their sofas in their living rooms or even their dining rooms, fearing that she has an incurable disease or she is covered in dirt that will contaminate their furniture.

She said worst of all; they order her around like she is their slave and talk to her like she is a piece of clay. She was surprised to see how these long-lost brothers and sisters treat the incoming Africans in such a hostile manner, and so she has been telling her people in Guinea about the hostility of these black Americans toward her and her Guinea people.

THE KENYAN RESPONDS

We spoke with a Kenyan lady, Esther, who has been living in St. Albans, Queens in New York. She informed us that black American women are the most beautiful women in the world because they have been mixed with all kinds of other races such as whites, Indians, Chinese and others, and so the color of black women comes in all shades, from light complexions to bronze, to Chinese look-alike to dark beauties.

She added that, as beautiful as they are, African men have no business marrying them, because they come from a society that looks condescendingly at the African. She said it is unconsciously difficult and almost impossible for black women to be submissive to African men since these women come from a society that believes the African is inferior and belittles him. She reiterated that it is a colossal and a monumental task for these black American women to be totally submissive and obey an African man that she inherently and unequivocally believes is a little lower than herself because of Tarzan and other negative documentaries depicting Africans as savages, barbarians, and uncivilized.

Esther pointed out to Africans that if the overwhelming majority of black American men were educated, financially stable, and drug free, the black American woman would never look at any African to even date them, let alone marry them, because they love, adore, and cherish their black men they bore, nurtured, and grew up with.

She said they marry the African out of sheer necessity because of the shortage of good black men in America. She said in her heart of hearts, many black women who marry an African know that they have ignored their hearts' desires and have married an inferior being, which secretly makes them unhappy and creates psychological problems and some elements of dysfunction in those marriages. She said because of the lopsidedness of such marriages, wherein the black woman maintains her superiority over the African, the women tend to dictate rules to the African men and want to have things their way, or else the marriage is fraught with incessant arguments and screaming. This is so because the black woman does not honestly, sincerely, and genuinely respect the African manhood, and therefore she does whatever she wants to please herself, regardless of whether it meets the approval of her husband or not. She said that because of her experience observing Africans married to black American women, she can definitely conclude that most black women merely tolerate their African husbands and they are in the marriage simply because of the shortage of eligible black men, period.

She said because of the absence of respect for their African husbands, there are a lot of conflicts between the couples, which result in endless arguments and unhappy relationships. This makes the African men begin to cheat or date other girlfriends to find happiness they are denied at home.

She added that most of the black American women in such marriages show a high degree of intolerance and impatience that makes them quick to anger. They do not necessarily listen to what their so-called inferior husbands are telling them, often saying to themselves, "What do these Africans know?"

FRANCIS FROM UGANDA NOTES

Francis, our friend from Kampala, Uganda also added that from anthropological and sociological perspective, many black Americans have inherited the ethnocentric bias prevalent in their society that their values, norms, and cultural beliefs are superior to the African, and consequently they behave condescendingly toward the African. He said because of this dichotomy in the perception of values and cultural beliefs, it a challenge and downright difficult for the black American to cooperatively and collaboratively interact with the African on an equal basis.

He said any relationship with their black American brothers and sisters inevitably deteriorates into lopsidedness with the blacks perceiving themselves, their mannerisms, outlooks, and way of life as inherently superior to the African's.

He added that the African, sensing the superior and a hostile attitude of these black American, ultimately annoys them and further perpetuates their separation. He said most Africans, therefore, feel comfortable dealing with the whites, who are more understanding of the Africans than the black Americans. Francis said this behavior explains why many Africans who are financially successful marry white women instead of the blacks.

He elaborated that most black Americans who view themselves as superior to Africans become jealous, envious, and hostile to see the so-called inferior Africans who come to America, discipline themselves to achieve success, and occupy higher professional positions than them.

Francis indicated that when Africans marry black American women, there are bound to be difficult challenges, which invariably destroys the relationships. He said these difficulties stem from the false premise of the black American belief of being superior to their African brothers and sisters. Additionally, Francis said Africans have the self-imposed discipline that prefers to save their monies for investments to acquire some level of financial security.

He contrasted this with the materialism of many black women who shop and spend lavishly, and are in credit card debt up to their eyeballs. He said this financial dichotomy is a major source of irritation and a potential for conflict in any relationship.

Francis indicated again that another potential irritant in an African-and-black-American marriage is that most of the black women have double standards; because they want to keep their friends they had before the marriage but resent the Africans having their friends come by to visit them. He said he has personally been to the home an African who was married to a black American whose mother was living with them, and when he asked the lady if she would allow her husband's mother to live with them, she exclaimed in anger that she would never in a million years allow that to happen!

Francis said another problem between the black American women who marry Africans is that they do not want their African husbands to go back to their jungle African nations.

Francis mentioned that often the African men do not really know that some of these black women are carrying heavy and serious life baggage. He said most of them may be coming out of abusive relationships with old husbands or boyfriends who impregnated them, did not take care of their children, and often were physically abusive to them. And therefore they are bitter and distrustful of men. The unsuspecting African who marries such women inherits all their suspicions, distrust of men, and confusion, and consequently goes through a nightmarish relationship.

Francis ended by saying that the Africans should be cautious and careful when dealing with black American women and not rush into any unwise relationships.

CAMEROONIAN PRINCETON GRADUATE REACTS

A Cameroonian, Dr. Mbah, who has lived in America for the past fifty years, asserted that white Americans view the black Americans as their competitors who are after their resources, their jobs, their white women, and are threats to their economic stability.

Dr. Mbah said the whites fear that someday these black Americans have the potential of carrying out a real revolution against them. He said the whites are uncomfortable because the black Americans were born right here in America and are too close to them. And if they allow them to have access to their white women, their race would be wiped out because offspring from any interracial relationships are black.

Dr. Mbah said the whites are afraid of the black man's violence, hostile demeanor, and their quick temper and rage. He said because of the whites' fear of black Americans, they have devised all forms of institutional racism or arrangements to keep them in their place and do not give them many opportunities to rise above their present condition.

He said the white man has devised a master plan to keep the blacks in their place, allowing only a handful to succeed in America. He said the whites give the black woman all kinds of opportunities to succeed because they are not so afraid of the black woman; hence, she is freer than her man.

Dr.Mbah contrasted the white man's treatment of the black American with that of the Africans. He said the whites do not consider the Africans a threat, because they are numerically few and come from a faraway place.

He said, moreover, the whites know that the Africans are glad to be in America and would not dare or are not in the position to challenge their hegemony. He added that most whites consider the African to be harmless, naïve, and generally good boys.

The whites also know that if the Africans get out of control, they could easily invoke immigration laws and deport them back to their countries of origin.

He said the whites therefore give many Africans the chance to succeed in America by giving them scholarships, offering them jobs, and even allowing some Africans to live with them because they are "good boys."

Dr.Mbah said many black Americans resent the Africans for the good treatment they receive in America—a treatment that they are denied, even though their ancestors worked, bled, sweat, and sacrificed to build America and their leaders like Rev. Martin Luther King, Abernathy, Andrew Young, and Jesse Jackson fought for civil rights in America. Most blacks view this as a clever ploy of the whites to play the Africans against them in the country of their birth and further resent the Africans for going along with such a vicious game against them.

Dr.Mbah said many black Americans are brainwashed to believe that Africans are inferior to them; hence, they do not truly accept them as their equals.

He added that many blacks are ignorant of African culture, politics, and progress, and many do not bother to learn anything about the African continent.

He added that most blacks would not even bother to invite the Africans to their homes, but many white people are quick to invite the Africans to their homes.

He said during the 1960 civil rights movement, which coincided with the independence of many African nations, many blacks finally discovered Africa and began identifying with African hairdos, dashikis, and some African leaders. He said many blacks loved the

African leaders who were notorious for killing whites, like the Mau Mau leader Jomo Kenyatta and General Idi Amin Dada.

He also said a lot of blacks identified with Ghana's president and dictator, Kwame Nkrumah, because of his virulent rhetoric against colonialism and imperialism but did not identify with most of the educated Africans living in America with them because they consider them as Uncle Toms.

REFLECTIONS ON SOME AFRICAN ORIGINS

It is important for us to remind the world that even though black Americans have lost most of their African values, morals, ethics, and traditions because of their forced transplantation into a new society; nevertheless the origins of most of their melodious soul music, their spirituality, and surprisingly most of their folktales are decidedly African.

Folktales in many African villages played a significant role in entertaining and imparting important cultural and traditional values and morals to children of most villages. Indeed these folktales preached their own lessons and were perhaps the most important cultural baggage that black Americans carried successfully in their heads to the new world. In the new world the blacks narrated the folktales in setting that were more or less similar to African, and they continue to do today.

Helena, a sixty-five-year-old lady from Greenville, South Carolina, informed us that during the evening, most of the people in their small town sat under or congregated under the peach, apple, or pear trees while the old folks began to narrate these folktales. These tales were for entertainment but sometimes "they gave us something or lessons to think about, and it helped us to use our minds to think to survive or think before you act," which is similar to what Africans do in all parts of the continent.

It is needless reiterating that because of their new conditions, social ostracism, and marginalization in the mainstream society, black Americans evolved and adapted their African folktales to suit their new conditions. Some of the old master, massa, massa king or master-john folktales shed ample light onto black American's evolution and adaptation of their folktales to reflect their master-servant humiliation; trauma; and abusive, lopsided conditions they were forced to endure for centuries in their new world.

It is significant to remind readers that black Americans did not emerge from the Atlantic Ocean; they came from Africa, and most of their folktales had African underpinnings, colorations, and indeed African roots in them, despite the deliberate intellectual dishonesty to disassociate their folktales from African origins.

The paramount or dominant characters that permeate African, West Indian, and black American folktales are the various ubiquitous tricksters referred to as Anansi, Spider, Rabbit or Brer Rabbit, and Tortoise, Fox or Brer Fox, or Hare, whose diabolical machinations or antics seem always to triumph in furtherance of their goals.

Juliana from Alabama narrated the folktale of Brer Rabbit and Uncle Remus from rural Alabama to us. This folktale, which is similar to many African trickster tales, began with Uncle Remus, who had a big vegetable farm that was nicely fenced. But Brer Rabbit dug a hole under the fence, and every night he would steal a lot of vegetables from the farm. Uncle Remus became tired of his vegetables being stolen from his farm, and so he set a trap and put some tar on the trap.

The next day when Uncle Remus came to his farm, he saw Brer Rabbit was stuck in the tar on the trap and said, "I got you now; I am going to throw you here in the bushes."

Brer Rabbit pleaded, "Please throw me anywhere, but not in the brier patch."

Uncle Remus was so angry he said, "Now I am going to throw you in that brier patch, and I do not care how much you plead with me." But poor Brer Rabbit kept pleading for him not to throw him in the brier patch. Uncle Remus threw him to the brier patch anyway.

Then Brer Rabbit laughed when he got into the brier patch and mocked Uncle Remus, saying that he was born and raised in the brier patch and this is where he wanted to go anyway.

Uncle Remus felt deceived by Brer Rabbit.

We discovered many of such trickster tales all through the southern United States from black Americans, and so after many years of separation from Africa, blacks still have in their folklore repertoire many authentic African folktales.

The antics of these Rabbit tales are narrated for entertainment and their morals are all over Africa. A favorite Ghanaian folktale about Rabbit, which is commonly narrated in many villages, informs us that Rabbit was similarly stealing the farm products of a rich farmer who decided to set a trap with liquid rubber.

The next day the Rabbit was caught by the trap of the farmer.

The same diabolical antics of Rabbit are seen in Kenya. In Sangora the deceitful Rabbit lies and cheats and deceives all the farmers and the king to steal all the groundnuts in their farms.

In Zimbabwe the clever scheming of Rabbit leads him to play on the intelligence of the crocodiles and made them stretch their backs for him to pretend to be counting them, while he indeed uses them to cross a large river with swift currents.

Despite many years of systematic and pernicious propaganda against black Americans to believe that Africa is uncivilized and a Dark Continent peopled as barbarians, blacks still spiritually retained many of their African traits.

EIGHT

CAN'T WE ALL GET ALONG?

Rodney King could not have said it any better: "Can't we all just get along?" Now, most of us remember what happened to Rodney King after his ugly ordeal and severe beatings by four or five policemen wielding batons. We remember their acquittal and the subsequent riots in Los Angeles. Throughout this ugly ordeal, Rodney king had it in his heart to proclaim that we should all be able to get along, which was beautiful gesture.

Now echoing the sentiments and humanity of Rodney King, we ask, how can the African and the black American get along? Do they really want to get along? Is it important for them to get along? Or is it true, as Omari from Cape Coast in, Ghana pessimistically prophesized, that nothing can bring the black American and the Africans together as long as the blacks erroneously believe they are superior to the African? Is he right or are the numerous good and God-fearing people from both sides prepared to challenge his and other nay-sayers pessimistic and distorted perceptions about Africans and blacks, and declare that it is imperative and essential for the African and the black American to come together for their mutual benefit and collective survival?

At this juncture it is instructive to remind these pessimists of the critical role of black Americans in the political decolonization of African countries. We should remind the world that Dr. W. E. B. DuBois was one of the founding organizers of the fifth Pan-African Congress in Manchester that produced great African nationalists like Kwame Nkrumah, Jomo Kenyatta, and others who spearheaded the independence of their respective nations.

Additionally we should remind our readers about the continuing leadership of Randall Robinson and his bold initiatives at his trans-Africa organization.

It is also significant to recall that it took only the comedian and activist Dick Gregory to single-handedly begin to demonstrate at the South African consulate against their apartheid regime. Because of his leadership it became fashionable and popular for all of us to join him in putting pressure on the odious government officials for the unconditional release of Nelson Mandela and the ultimate dismantling of the apartheid government.

Again, the tireless black warrior of our era, the indomitable Rev. Jesse Jackson, toured African countries explaining the black condition to African politicians and diplomats, and returned to American to champion the name change of his people from black Americans to African Americans.

We should not also discount the bold and impressive leadership of the Rev. Al Sharpton during the sad days after the senseless murder of a West African immigrant Amadu Diallo in New York City, and countless numerous black Americans who have substantially contributed to the progress and development of Africans on the continent.

Those of us who are deeply religious want to emulate the example of Joseph in the Bible, who preceded his brothers to Egypt through divine preordination to save his brothers from hunger and destruction.

The question on our minds is, were the black Americans divinely placed here in America centuries ago to save their African brethren from extinction? Is the black American ordeal in America a deliberate divine intervention or plan to save the black race from extinction or from some great unfathomable purpose that is unknowable to us? Are the black Americans the chosen people to redeem the African continent? Were the blacks selected or chosen to learn the secrets of modern civilization from the white man and to replicate them on the African continent to save the entire continent from hunger, poverty, and destruction? Do you also believe that the Almighty God allowed the blacks to undergo such a painful ordeal so that nothing good would come out of it? Do you sincerely believe that God allowed or permitted black people to be carried from their homes in Africa, through the painful middle passage to America to be enslaved for more than 200 years for nothing?

We strongly believe that there is a divine plan for black Americans to fulfill, whether we know it or not, because our wisdom is like a child's compared to the ways and wisdom of the Almighty God. Since we are convinced that there is an absolute divine plan for black Americans with respect to Africa, like the role of Joseph in Egypt, how can the Africans and the black Americans get together without all these acrimonies, hostilities, animosities, fake superiorities, and inferiorities? What can we do to begin the healing process? And believe us; no human being on both sides, however pessimistic he may be, can prevent the unfolding of a divine plan by God. And for the overwhelmingly majority of blacks in America and Africa who want to move with the divine flow of the East meeting the West, join us in seeking ways or methods that can enhance this togetherness—that are sure to break barriers.

In the prophetic words of President Ronald Reagan, "tear down this evil wall" of separation between the Africans and their black American brothers and sisters.

How do we tear down this century-old wall of intolerance, ignorance, and hostility between our two peoples?

TAKING A RETROSPECTIVE GLANCE

Reverend Jones of a Baptist church in New York City said Africans need to understand what the blacks have been through in America to be able to fully understand their behavior and why they have the attitudes they currently have. He said Africans should understand that the slave trade that forcibly captured and separated Africans from their loved ones—their mothers, fathers, and extended family—constitute a hostile act in the collective memory of the slaves and their descendants.

He said the African slaves were further shipped into hostile nations, where the slaves were denied their freedoms and were whipped until the lashes were stamped on their flesh where blood oozed out.

He said when the African slaves spoke their native language; their tongues were plucked or cut out. He said the African slaves were abused, treated like animals, and forced by the threat of horrible deaths to abandon their African names, folktales, songs, and anything that identified them with Africa.

He said these abuses that forced black Americans to abandon their African culture collectively made the blacks distance themselves from anything African. He said they had to distance themselves from Africa if they wanted to live their lives without any harm coming to them.

He reminded us that if you see black Americans who do not identify with Africa, it is because they were collectively forced by the threat of death to abandon the African culture, and he added, "What you see today are the remnants of the of the work done to their minds yesterday." He said black Americans must begin to reconnect with their African roots by learning the authentic African traditions; but the problem is, where do they even begin to learn about African culture? He said traditional black colleges and universities must make the study of African folklore, proverbs, festivals, art, and crafts a must in their core requirements for graduation to give the black college student an appreciation of his or her ancestral background.

The Rev. Jones reminded us that even after the slaves were freed there were barbarous lynchings of more than 5,000 black Americans all over the South. He said the lynching of the black man was like a community affair where neighbors and friends were happily invited and some trains and buses even gave discount tickets to the eager and happy spectators. And some sold souvenirs to the cheering crowds, among whom were numerous Christians. He said during the actual lynching ceremony the black man had the rope around his neck and was hanged to the applause of the cheering whites, some of whom were taunting and calling him names, saying, "nigger die, nigger die." And after the hanging, whether he was pronounced dead or not, these cheering crowds set a fire underneath him and slowly cooked him into charred remains.

Rev. Jones said these barbarous tortures that black Americans were subjected to for more than a century put a lot of fear into them—fear that stifled the initiative, drive, ambitions, motivations, and spirit of achievement of numerous black Americans.

He said many of the blacks who were lynched were progressive and accomplished black men and women and that the majority of whites did not want to see them progress. He asked what you think such humiliating and dreadful acts of torture did to the self-esteem and aspirations of the blacks. He added that these acts of barbarism are etched into the collective memory of black Americans and have served to damage the collective psyche of many black men, and it would take a lot of healing to restore them to their real selves.

Rev. Jones said this psychological damage to the collective psyche of black Americans was deepened and intensified because of forced segregation, when blacks were ostracized from all white areas and forbidden to drink from the same water fountain as whites. They were forced to sit at the back of public buses and were not allowed to attend the same schools as the whites. He added that the blacks were forced to believe that they were inferior and unclean human beings.

He said that after many years of such treatment some blacks began to believe in the dominant society's power of suggestion and unconsciously began to behave like the dominant white society wanted them to. He said the African should understand that black Americans fought and died in numerous civil demonstrations before they were reluctantly allowed to attend the same schools as whites. He added that it was in the 1960s even state-sponsored colleges and universities, which black people's taxes, were used to support, allowed blacks to attend because of court decisions.

Rev. Jones said Africans should indeed be grateful to the black Americans for fighting vigorously against Jim Crow laws in America to enable them to come from their countries to enjoy these institutions today. He said for the Africans and black Americans to come together, the incoming Africans must not take the blacks for granted, because they paved the way with their sweat and blood for the Africans to see the little privileges available to them in America today.

He said the Africans owe the black Americans a huge debt of gratitude for the work and sacrifices they have made in America to make it possible for the African to come here to educate himself, get a job, set up businesses, or to be able to remit some funds to help their kith and kin on the continent of Africa—remittances that go a long way to helping develop the entire African continent.

Rev. Jones said the Africans coming to American today still sense and smell the lingering institutional and subtle racism prevalent in the society. He said the Africans are getting a small taste of what the blacks have been subjected to all their lives. He added that police in various states do racial profiling of all blacks, including Africans, and they kill African men like Amadou Diallo, just like they do black men, and real estate redline all black men, including Africans.

He reminded Africans to organize community celebrations and invite as many black Americans as they possibly can to thank them for all they have done and endured to pave the way for them. He said African and black scholars can organize discussion forums and have discussions about this and other issues to develop the modalities of the coming together of our two peoples. He said churches and community groups should endeavor to invite Africans to participate in discussions where black scholars, intellectuals, clergymen, and community leaders can explain the historical significance of black experience in America to the Africans.

He added that such an experience will serve to make the Africans understand what the blacks have been through in America and make them appreciate the importance of black Americans. Those who look down upon the blacks, those that thumb their noses at the blacks; and those that ignore the blacks will know that they owe a substantial debt of gratitude to the black Americans. He said such a realization would begin the long, winding road of healing between "our two peoples."

Rev. Jones also encouraged the educated talented Africans, telling them to go back to their respective countries and help develop their nations with their expertise. He added that when many black Americans see that Africans are going back to their countries to help develop their nations, some of them with skills will begin to assist them by accompanying some of them to Africa, like many black people did when Kwame Nkrumah returned to Ghana to help with the decolonization and rebuilding of his nation.

Rev. Jones further asserted that Africans and black Americans should not make assumptions about each other, should not have preconceived and prejudicial notions about each other, and should approach each other with clean minds, willing to learn about experiences from each other.

He said blacks and Africans should not believe the negative indoctrinations and the hostile propaganda of people who profited from their miseries, abused them like animals, and continue to discriminate against them to pit them against each other. He said Africans and black Americans should begin to establish a clear line of communication and increase interactions with each other to dispel the myths we have about each other.

He said the greatest obstacle between the African and the black American is that "we are ignorant of each other, and we let other people who do not have our interest at heart dictate and influence our thinking of how we should interact with each other."

Finally the Rev. Jones said increased intermarriage between the blacks and Africans will help cement the relationship and give our peoples a firm foothold. He said for such marriages to be beneficial to our race, the Africans should not to pretend to marry the black women because of their quest for green cards to stay in America, but they should marry them because they genuinely love them, want to learn from each other, and treat the black women like long-lost African queens who are being newly discovered.

OUR COMMON DESTINY?

Nana Kofi Ayeribi, odikuro, or chief, of the small town Koodum near Akwasiho in the eastern region of Ghana, has intimated that black Americans and Africans have a common destiny and must learn to come together and work to resolve their common problems.

He informed us that it is weird or strange for the black Americans to look down on the African—to have negative perceptions of Africa, to still believe that Africans are cannibals, savages, and primitives. He said no matter what the blacks believe, they still came from Africa, and so Africa is their roots, and it is very unwise for them to have negative perceptions of their roots. He said those who have these negative attitudes toward their roots are not securely anchored to the ground, and anybody in their correct and healthy mind would love and cherish the very foundation, or roots, that anchor them to their ground for them to maintain their stability and firmness.

Nana said an orange tree couldn't love only the succulent and tasty oranges it bears and turns around and look down or think negatively about its roots that support and anchor it to the ground.

He advised if the orange tree perceived its roots negatively, the tree would poison or sour the main work of its roots and in time would poison its succulent oranges on the tree. Nana said there is an absolute necessity and an almost a dire imperative for the black American to reconnect with his rich roots to gain the immense amount of benefits that lay quietly awaiting his recognition.

Nana said that like the orange tree, black Americans who perceive their African roots negatively will continue to sour their beautifully ripened, succulent, and tasty oranges, and will begin to have problems with themselves, their wives, their affairs, and even their children because the negative perception of their roots reflects on themselves and on their affairs. Nana said those who believe that their ancestors are savages, cannibals, and inferior are actually saying to themselves and their loved ones that they themselves are still savages, cannibals, and inferior and deserve all the problems implicit in such beliefs.

Nana said when black American boys and girls make rap songs and start calling their mothers and sisters "bitches," "whores," and all kinds of unprintable words, then you know that the oranges are not only poisoned but soured.

He said when some black mothers go on crack and other drug binges and abandon their babies in crack dens; you know the oranges have indeed soured. He said when many of our very intelligent black American boys and girls, who are as brilliant as sunshine, would waste all their precious time in the streets as gangsters selling drugs and murdering each other instead of going to college; then you know that those fine oranges are indeed very poisoned and need to reconnect with their roots for transformation and regeneration.

Nana added that when almost the entire prison population in America is overwhelmingly black Americans boys and a growing number of black girls, then we definitely know that the oranges are not only sour but are about to be damaged and need desperately to reconnect to their roots to find out the remedy to reverse their current trend of affairs.

Nana Ayirebi called on all Africans and black Americans to establish Africa Day celebrations in all parts of Africa and black American cities, a celebration that will involve blacks on both sides of the Atlantic.

He said the yearly African Day celebrations could coincide with the Juneteen anniversaries celebrated all over black neighborhoods in America, during which there are all kinds of activities planned by a committee of responsible African and black American elders with the ostensible motives for bringing our two peoples together.

Some of the celebrations would include historical discussions of great Africans and black Americans and their contributions to our people. During these celebrations, the highest African and black American medals of Honor should be bestowed upon people of our race who have contributed to make our collective lives a little easier.

He added that during these celebrations, black American historians, activists, and other eminent spokesmen of our race should educate Africans from the continent about the life of the black American in American society, and vice versa. He said that during these celebrations, Africans and their black American counterparts would be able to discuss business linkages of mutual benefit to them.

RADIO AND TELEVISION IMAGERY

For hundreds of years there has been a deliberate and orchestrated propaganda war against Africa through negative imagery, stereotyping, and false representation of Africa to the black American through movies, cartoons, documentaries, magazines, and intellectual journals that caricatured the African as a subhuman and inferior species.

To reverse this false media representation of Africans and black Americans, media experts from both sides have to join hands to purchase television rights, advertisements, and radio and newspaper campaigns aimed at portraying the reality: both the good and bad of Africa and black America. It is needless reiterating to say that black Americans have been subjected to negative and false media representation, casting them as criminals and clowns in the popular media.

We are aware of the changing trends, but more needs to be done. It behooves all of us to get on the media bandwagon and help correct these media distortions of our people, which foster low self-esteem among our people, and to portray the reality of our people to the world—both the ugly and the good.

We desperately appeal to great black movie talents like Spike Lee, Singleton, and the rest to consider making movies wherein Africans are positively portrayed to the black American audience.

In an alliance to correct the falsity and distorted propaganda against all black people in the world, our Afro-centric scholars must endeavor to challenge the false premise of the Judeo-Christian interpretation of history that seeks to whitewash the evils of slavery.

Such interpretations aggressively seek to shower the entire blame of the trans-Atlantic slave trade squarely on the African shoulders, erroneously blaming the Africans for selling their brothers and sisters into slavery and subjecting the Africans to the displeasure of black Americans, making them inwardly resent the African.

Our Afro-centric scholars must continue to build upon the great and monumental classic work of Chancellor Williams in the destruction of black civilizations and the incisive and revealing works of prolific scholars like John Henrik Clarke, Josef ben-Jochannan, J.A. Rogers, Leonard Jefferies, Cheikh Anta Diop, Molefi Kete Asante, and others. These Afro-centric writings and others must challenge the false premise of Africans selling their kith and kin into the slave trade. Africans and black Americans must seek out most of these powerful writers to reeducate themselves about the facts of the trans-Atlantic slave trade.

PUBLIC APOLOGY TO BLACK AMERICANS?

Even though we have emphatically and categorically denied the assertions of many black Americans that Africans sold them into the trans-Atlantic slave trade, it is probable that the entire slave trade would not have been as successful as it was had there not been some element of complicity on the part of some powerful African chiefs and their advisers who saw a means of enriching themselves.

Additionally it could also be entirely possible that certain powerful tribal groups could not resist the temptation of maneuvering to collude with the slave traders to rid themselves of hostile tribes.

Because of these constant naggings from black Americans about the complicity of certain African chiefs in the slave trade that sent our dear brothers and sisters to a strange land where all kinds of unimaginable abuses were visited upon them, Africans must take the initiative to begin the difficult process of healing these raw and open wounds.

Of course these healing processes have different dimensions, but most concerned Africans and black Americans strongly advocate that African leaders, their chiefs, and other people should organize a month-long period of healing in Africa, where the Africans and their leaders will publicly apologize for whatever role they played in the slave trade.

These public apologies, in the form of resolutions signed by all participating leaders and witnessed by black American leaders, should be sent to all black churches, Moslem mosques, black schools, newspapers, magazines, and television and radio shows. We sincerely believe that such a public apology will show a good-faith effort on the part of the African people for genuine reconciliation with their black American brothers and sisters, which would contribute substantially to the healing process between both peoples. Perhaps when the main culprits of this odious trade, the Europeans, see Africans making a public apology to black Americans, it will bring out their humanity and moral correctness and they will see the necessity of making a public apology to black Americans and begin to genuinely heal the pain that many of them suffer today.

This public apology should also be the starting point of teaching black children the true history of the greatness of the black race, and it should mark the beginning of the gradual dismantling of white supremacists' teachings and bravado, which we have all become accustomed to over the years.

ESTABLISHMENT OF SLAVE HOLOCOUST MUSEUMS

By establishing the holocaust museum, the Jewish people and their leadership have set a monumental example by making sure that future generations do not forget their holocaust experience during the lunacy of Adolf Hitler and his racist henchmen in their systematic annihilation of over six million Jews.

Yes, we agree that the Jewish peoples' examples in building these holocost museums and of course the prophetic warnings of the Harvard educated philosopher George Santayana that those who do not learn from history are doomed to repeat its mistakes.

We call upon our ancestors, particularly those who perished in the horrible middle passages, to spiritually guide our people to establish slave holocaust museums all over the west coast of Africa and inselected American cities.

These holocaust museums can also house black American cultural exchange centers, where scholars from both sides of the Atlantic can learn from each other. Here African languages, dance, religion, arts, crafts, folklore, proverbs and authentic Afro-centric oral and written historical information about African can be researched and disseminated abroad.

These holocaust museums will be a lasting reminder of what our people have endured for centuries under the stranglehold of the Europeans.

THE ROLE OF BLACK CHURCHES

Africans living in America should at all costs endeavor to join black churches and actively and faithfully participate in some of the churches' committees or activities. African families in those churches must make it a point to invite some of their black American families to dinners or parties and learn from each other to reduce the high level of suspicion by talking and explaining their ways of life and preparation of meals to each other.

The churches can host several cultural awareness weeks, where Africans and black Americans can display their cultural and traditional ways of doing things: their artifacts, foods, clothes, arts and crafts. And Africans can explain these traditions to interested participants who genuinely want to know and understand some of the African cultural benefits.

Africans must also ask the blacks to explain their way of doing things and learn from them. Attempts must be made to explain marriage counseling. A committee in the churches comprised of Africans and black marriage counselors should intercede into cross-cultural marriages between blacks and Africans to educate them to learn and respect each other's way of life.

The churches should also have symposium and discussion groups centered around the Bible on how to bring these diverse people with different backgrounds together as one family with love and understanding.

Africans living in black communities should actively participate in their neighborhood community organizations and not be intimidated by what some blacks and other arrogant Africans might say or do, like even laughing at their accents. Community groups must also sponsor different discussion groups, symposia, and debates about the Africans and the black Americans' perceptions of each other.

These discussions should not necessarily involve only the celebrities, but ordinary people must be encouraged to participate in them to expose their ideas and fears to the groups and be enlightened by others.

We believe that through these associations black Americans and Africans can begin the healing process and learn, among other things, what each group hates and dislikes, and the common ground for each group to build on. Some blacks and Africans can develop business contacts from these associations.

We have to commend the pioneering efforts of all the African poetry theatres all over the nation for sponsoring African cultural events, dances, art exhibitions, language lessons, fashion shows and other numerous Afro-centric activities and lectures. We salute them for their foresight, courage, and leadership.

In 1985 to1986 our coauthor Kwame taught the Twi language, spoken in Ghana, at the African Poetry Theater in Queens, New York to a group of black Americans visiting Ghana to perform cultural activities.

The churches should also attempt to sponsor revivals and conventions on many African countries to teach African religiosity and remove the notion that religions in Africa are simply voodoos.

The black churches can design programs and work closely with the criminal justice system to sponsor at-risk adolescents and preadolescents who are teetering on the brink of delinquency so they can attend boarding schools in Africa, which will enable them graduate from high schools and colleges before returning to America.

THE ROLE OF EDUCATION

It is equally important for black American teachers from elementary schools through high schools and colleges to be granted a one-year sabbatical to an African university to participate in or attend various classes to learn about the reality and truth about Africa. Such an adventure will broaden the outlook of these teachers, which will positively impact their teaching of black American children when they return home.

Africans in America should endeavor to enroll in traditional black colleges to pursue their undergraduate academic degrees. This experience will expose the Africans to the traditions of the black Americans.

There should also be an increase of black American exchange students attending selected African colleges and universities to enable them study and earn their undergraduate degrees and broaden their societal orientation and outlook so they will understand that Africans are not living with Tarzan, Jane, and cheetah.

Black American families should also participate in hosting African students for a year and should help reeducate them in a black worldview or teach them about the reality and the condition of the black American. In this same atmosphere of friendship, cooperation, and cordiality, African families all over the continent should also sponsor black American students for a year to study in Africa to learn about the reality of the African life.

The African governments must attempt to establish senior citizen assisted living facilities in Africa to attract interested black retirees who want to settle in warm climates. The black Americans retirees who choose to participate in such a program can benefit in a number of ways. For one thing, most loneliness that plagues black elderly people will be gone because they will be in a community of their peers and will be living in a city within a city, complete with all kinds of caretakers, and transportation and medical facilities.

The African countries will also benefit from these arrangements, because most of the skilled retirees like doctors, technicians, electricians, pharmaceutical experts, and the others will bring their expertise to teach the growing number of Africans who can utilize these skills to benefit their society.

An African American female, also suggested that the rites of passage (much like the Jewish barmitzpah), wherein African elders instill discipline in their youngsters, should be instituted in black schools, churches, neighborhood organizations, and other black-oriented associations.

She suggested that such an arrangement will involve African chiefs traveling to American once a year to perform these rites through their folktales, proverbs, and other oral traditions that will serve to instill discipline and respect for the elderly, particularly in black American boys. She further added that the first initiates will teach the rites of passage to other black boys to perpetuate such knowledge.

African governments must at all costs continue to encourage tourism to their countries, but should make it more attractive to black Americans to visit their countries. College students who visit these countries must be accommodated for free at the local university dormitories during the summer months when school is not in session. This gesture will encourage many black Americans to visit African countries to broaden their outlook.

YOUTH MOVEMENTS

Young people are the future of our race for both the African and the black American; it is therefore significant for them to have important, friendly movements that will help link them together for their mutual benefit.

Such friendly movements can include music festivals where Africans and black Americans get together to display and perform the music of both continents and also add lyrics to their rap songs that make fun of the escapades of Tarzan, Jane, and cheetah in Africa; and the negative documentaries about black people. They should include more positive messages in their rap lyrics that will help uplift the self-esteem of our young folks on both sides of the Atlantic.

During the summer months, interested African governments can sponsor some interested black American teenagers to spend the entire summer in their countries to learn about the nature of their governments, the life of their people, the culture of the natives (including the oral and written histories), and other places of interest to the youngsters.

Similarly, African teenagers can also be invited to the traditional black colleges to attend summer schools and camps all throughout the South to learn more about the blacks, their history, and American experience.

During the independence celebrations of African nations, selected black American students should be invited to participate in their celebrations. Such participations will help the black youngsters learn more about these countries, the meaning and significance of the independence to our race, and the political history of those African countries.

Once again, thanks to globalization, we live in a virtual global village today, where the Worldwide Web enables all humanity to surf the entire globe. All African countries now have their own Web sites, and interested black Americans can get all the information and knowledge of African nations by visiting their Web sites.

BLACK AMERICAN EXPERIMENT IN GHANA?

At this juncture it is pertinent to take a cursory retrospective glance at the black American homecoming to Ghana between 1960 and 1966. Valerie Melissa Babb, a professor of African American Studies at the University of Georgia wrote:

> From 1960-1966 Ghana represented a complex intertwining of place and identity. For a people whose cultural memory included the forced traversing of Atlantic, returning to Ghana was imagined as a reverse transiting providing a starting point from which to make sense of slavery and subsequent black identity.
> The deposing of Nkrumah in 1966 forced the exodus of many of these black migrants from their all-too-fleeting "utopia'. Angelou captures their sentiment and disillusionment when she writes, "Many of us had only begun to realize in Africa that the Stars and Stripes was our flag and our only flag, and that knowledge was almost too painful to bear."
> Though this community is not remembered in the ways, that Paris or Harlem might be, nonetheless it captured the attempts of black Americans and others to establish a politically powerful African homeland. The reach of Ghana renaissance went past the brief sojourn of its residents. Their dream of a new world is still very much a part of the black imagination, and the vision they helped refine and disseminate still constitutes a powerful draw for modern seekers. 7

Most of us who are working feverishly for the reunification of blacks in diasporas with the Africans on the continent applaud and commend the almost superhuman efforts of these brave black souls who ventured into a nation unknown to them and left their comfortable and established professions in their more developed society to come to Africa to start life all over again.

It is unfortunate that most of them left Ghana after the demise of Kwame Nkrumah's government, but this should serve as a significant lesson to contemporary African governments that one man should not have such awesome dictatorial powers, which Nkrumah assumed in Ghana, but must create competing, pluralistic, and decentralized institutions for the populace. The coup, or a change of the administration in power, should not have had such dire, dramatic, and negative societal consequences and a deterioration leading to the exodus of black Americans and other professionals whose mission was to assist the people of Ghana and establish a homeland for themselves.

It is also pertinent for African governments to consider extending dual citizenships to black American professionals interested in Africa and allow those who want to participate in the political process of these nations to stay, allowing those interested to run for political offices and genuinely seek to seriously integrate themselves into their societies.

We were a little surprised, though, that those black Americans who surrounded Kwame Nkrumah could not or perhaps did not challenge or forcefully and candidly advice him to set up a truly egalitarian and democratic political system devoid of his many intolerant political excesses of establishing preventive detention acts that allowed him to jail his opponents without trials.

Those black Americans who surrounded Nkrumah should have known that because of the dictatorial and coercive policies of Nkrumah, the average Ghanaian was reduced to a slave in his own land, and it was only a matter of time before the freedom-loving Ghanaians would get his madness out of their nation, which has nothing to do with the black Americans residing in the nation.

The lesson here though is that the incoming black Americans should not identify totally with only the party or government in power but should identify with the ordinary people in the African nations and seek to integrate themselves with the people and the various community groups of these societies, and not the necessarily the government that is here today and gone tomorrow.

Also, there is this nagging uneasiness among many Africans that some black Americans have become identified with the activities of American Central Intelligence Agency (CIA) and deliberately identify and mingle with Africans only to spy on them to obtain all kinds of sensitive governmental and other information that is ultimately used to undermine African governments.

Former Ghanaian President Kwame Nkrumah lamented bitterly after the 1966 coup overthrew his government, and complained about the role of the black American ambassador in Accra. He wrote:

It is alleged that the U.S. Ambassador, Franklin Williams, offered the traitors 13 million dollars to carry out a coup d'etat. Afrifa, Harley and Kotoka were to get a large share of this if they would assassinate me at Accra airport as I prepared to leave for Hanoi. I understand Afrifa said: "I think I will fail", and declined the offer. So apparently did the others.

It is particularly disgraceful that it should have been an Afro-American ambassador who sold himself out to the imperialists and allowed himself to be used in this way. It was this same man who deliberately lied when he publicly described the coup as "bloodless." However, his treachery provides a sharp reminder of the insidious ways in which the enemies of Africa can operate. In the U.S.A. the "Uncle Tom" figure is well known. We have mercilessly seen less of him in Africa. 8

It is significant to note that Kwame Nkrumah was not the only person making these negative insinuations against black Americans, but many researchers and observers of the African political scene confirm these nagging suspicions.

For example, Ronald Kessler reveals the involvement of a black American colluding with the CIA:

> Sharon M. Scranage was a thirty-year-old operations support for the CIA in Ghana. She gave classified information to her Ghanaian boyfriend, Michael Soussoudis, a first cousin of Jerry Rawlings. She handed Soussoudis virtually everything there was to know about the CIA activities in Ghana.... Her spying led to the compromise of eight CIA agents who were arrested and imprisoned. The CIA has resettled in the U.S. nearly two dozen Ghanaians, including families, who were compromised as a result of the fiasco. 9

Many Africans are wondering why some black Americans work with their former slave masters against Africans, and they wonder if Africans can sincerely trust them as their true brothers and sisters. Should black Americans be surprised when Africans become suspicious of them? But of course not all black Americans in African work for the CIA, because there are many ordinary, innocent blacks who come to Africa for many different reasons and have nothing to do with any government activities, and the few agents make it difficult for the rest of the innocent ones there to enjoy the society.

However, it is needless reiterating to state that many native Africans are also spies for the CIA, as in the case of the two dozen Ghanaian CIA agents who had to be resettled in the United States because they were CIA agents. Africans cannot say black Americans are working against them when their own Africans are also colluding with the CIA.

Even in the case of Kwame Nkrumah's coup, Nkrumah can blame Franklin Williams all he wants, but it took the members of the native Ghanaian armed forces colluding with the CIA to actually overthrow his government. It was not just the black Americans alone spying on Kwame Nkrumah, but many native Ghanaians were involved in the pernicious plot against him, and most of the high-level Ghanaian elites were reportedly on the CIA payroll. Generally, therefore, we cannot blame only the black Americans and be suspicious of them, but we have to look at the diabolical machinations of the native Africans colluding with foreign intelligence networks against African governments.

Again, having lived in foreign lands for well over thirty years, we are painfully aware of the problems and difficulties many foreigners encounter in a new society, as Valerie Melissa Babb noted:

> "Though her autobiography celebrates connections between old world and new, Angelou's characterization of Ghana is by no means nostalgic. She reveals the limits of Diasporic idealism in remembering the indifference or resistance of some of Accra's community to the Afros, and ultimately realizes, 'We could physically return to Africa, find jobs, learn languages, even marry and remain on African soil all our lives, but we were born in the United States which held the graves of our grandmothers and grandfathers.'" 10

It is significant to note that part of the indifferences some black Americans encountered in Ghana and in some West Africans nations revolve around the concept of racism or the hostile treatment that black Americans have experienced in America.

It is an understatement for us to assert that the black American experience in America is colored primarily by the hostile racial discrimination. The abusive treatment black Americans have gone through and continue to go through today is beyond description.

Black Americans have endured the wrath of a white racist society in America and were ostracized or segregated from the mainstream society, discriminated against in every sector of the society; and have endured every conceivable abuse meted to them.

Even though the federal government has remedied several egregious wrongs against blacks, the overt discrimination against them in some parts of the nation has gone underground to become subtle institutional racism. We cannot begin to write about the nature of the hostile treatment and discrimination blacks continue to endure in America today.

It defies the comprehension of the average black African who has not traveled to America or parts of Western Europe that black people are subjected to all kinds of hostile racial discrimination because of the color of their skin, which the Almighty God, in his infinite wisdom, gave them.

These black Africans cannot conceive that these same white people, who act very nice, smile, talk politely and act like angels to them in West Africa and other parts of Africa, behave in a wicked and mean-spirited way toward black people in America.

The black American who goes to any West African country to explain the racist and the mean-spirited nature of whites' treatment of black people will be very frustrated by the "indifference" of the natives.

Africans will look at blacks dumbfounded, like they are crazy, and some may wonder whether the blacks are crazy or drunk, because the black African living in his native land cannot conceptualize what racism actually is or does and how it affects the livelihood of black people in America. Those who have not traveled to live in white countries may read and hear about racism, and on occasion may use those racist expressions, but do not understand the emotional connotative impact of those words. The African does not understand what it means to live and experience life in a racist society—the horrible inhumanity of racism, the wickedness, the painful dehumanization, and the utter disregard and disdain for the humanity of black people who dwell among whites.

The black African cannot understand the concept of the arrogance of the white supremacists and their daily condescension and menacing treatment of black people living in their countries, albeit the constant harassment of white police officers and their often violent physical abuse of black people in their custody.

The black African who lives in Africa does not understand this boldfaced, wicked racism that black Americans endure on daily basis in America and elsewhere in Europe because of many reasons:

- Even though Africans were colonized, the Europeans ruled mostly by employing the shrewd method of indirect rule, using some African chiefs and Africans themselves to administer, oppress, and exploit the natives. These Africans became the new elites of their people and were proud of their new positions under the white men. They indeed became the obedient boys of the empire and loved the white man so much so that in Ghana Dr. Kofi Busia wrote to the Queen of England that Ghana was not ready for freedom from England. Now, tell me how much discussion can a black American who has suffered years of racial discrimination in America have with such an African scholar from Oxford? This naïve concept of racism among the black Africans is different in South Africa, where the whites ruled for hundreds of years under the odious, defunct, and barbaric apartheid regime.

- The population of the white people living in many parts of West Africa and in other so-called sub-Saharan countries is extremely small or insignificant compared to the millions of the black Africans. Like Richard Pryor—the late comedian—used to joke, in black Africa white people look out for each other because everybody is black. Because white people are a small minority in many African countries and are not in overt political power, they are for the most part very diplomatic, cordial, pleasant, nice, personable, and go through inordinate lengths to be nice to the native Africans. The natives, for their part, love and respect the humanity of the white people, treat them kindly and respectfully, and would go to any length to cater to the white people in their countries; and they would never believe that these same white people mistreat, abuse, and look down upon black people as inferior beings because of the black skin God gave them.

- The role of the missionaries and Christian evangelists in West Africa in softening the hearts of the natives is instructive here. These missionaries and evangelists bombarded and continue to bombard the natives with the so-called good news: to love thy neighbor as thyself; do unto others as you want done unto you; blessed are the meek for they shall inherit the earth; love your enemies; forgive people that hurt and offend thee seven times seventy seven; and blessed are those that are merciful to others because God will be merciful to them. These and other disarming messages from the Bible, which many of these missionaries and the Christian evangelists do not actually practice in their native countries, are pumped into the naïve minds of most Africans, who emotionally and literally believe these things and take them to heart. The sad irony is that many Africans actually believe in their hearts that many white people believe and practice these teachings in their relationships with black people, until they come to American and other European countries to live and realize that many white people do not believe in the Christian ethics and teachings when it comes to their treatment of and dealings with black people. A case of a group of new foreign students from Cameroon illustrates and amplifies this point. These Cameroonian students were new college students in Missouri and were devout Catholics eager to fellowship with the Catholic "brothers". When these new Cameroonians informed Kwame of their desire to attend the Catholic Church, he warned them not to attend all-white churches in the middle of the Ozarks, because the abiding racism there blinds many of the Christians not to warmly embrace black Christians. They did not believe Kwame, because they deeply believe what the missionaries and the Christian evangelists preached to them in the Cameroon, and so they went to the all-white Catholic Church. When these new Cameroonians attended the church, they experienced a form of humiliation they were not prepared for, because during the communion the entire congregation drank from a common big cup. But after the new Cameroonian students drank from the cup, none of the rest of the white congregation drank after them. The rest of the white catholic brothers and sisters absolutely refused to drink from the same cup these "inferior, unclean" Cameroonians students drank from. Needless to say, these students felt humiliated and were never the same again, because they had experienced what black Americans had been trying to tell them about. They would never have understood what any black American told them until they experienced it for themselves.

- Most black Africans live in material and financial poverty, and most need the white man to help provide jobs and aid to assist them. Hence, many look up to the great white man to help them. The last thing on their minds is that this same white man is a racist, and so when the black American informs the African of the white racists, the African responds "but I need this racist to survive" and therefore becomes indifferent to him.

- Conversely, the whites in Africa also need the Africans to work in their mines and businesses; hence, they are understandably diplomatic to them because common sense dictates to them that they have to be civil and treat the natives nicely if they are to continue to peacefully exploit the abundant resources in Africa.

- The Africans are more concerned about the lingering effects of tribalism, like the Ibos and the Hausas, the Akans and the northerners in Ghana, and the southern Christians and Moslems hostilities in Ivory Coast, than the white people's racism. Indeed many of the African natives view the whites as a breath of fresh air and are not concerned about their racist nature, because the whites don't openly practice it among the natives, even though secretly in their hearts they look condescendingly upon them as barbaric and uncivilized people.

It is indeed understandably frustrating to the black American that generally the black African, except of course the South African blacks, does not understand what racism is in practice, which makes it appear that the black African is indifferent to black Americans' suffering and racial discrimination. But please forgive many of them because they do not have a clue about actual racism until they have experienced it in white countries, like the shooting of an unarmed Guinean immigrant by four armed policeman who pumped thirty-two bullets into his body and were subsequently set free by their brothers for self-defense.

These indifferences and resistances that Maya Angelou and her people encountered in Ghana cannot be swept easily under the rug as culture shock. We sincerely believe that a well-thought-out cultural education in schools and on radio and television, as well as activities for both newcomers and native Africans, would help erode some of these resistances and would gradually bring about a cementation of these fragile relationships, which will make the incoming black Americans feel at home in their adopted African societies.

Also, both the black American and the African must be reoriented to have a new attitude of genuine respect, brotherhood, sisterhood, and a real agape love for each other.

To this end, African merchants must be trained not to charge exorbitant prices or deliberately overcharge black Americans who purchase their products, and they must learn to treat them like their own brothers and sisters.

It is important also that black Americans do not give their hard-earned monies to the natives and expect that they will be entirely honest in procuring lands and other business deals for them. In the past many natives have duped many unsuspecting black Americans.

The best thing for the prospective black American businessman to do is register his business with the requisite government agency and obtain legal counsel to assist him in his business encounters in Africa.

It is also unadvisable for him to allow the natives to count the local currency for him, but he must learn to understand the local currencies to avoid being cheated by the natives.

Similarly, black Americans must also not go to Africa with a superior attitude and look condescendingly at the locals, but must have genuine respect and eagerness to learn from their brothers and sisters on the continent. And they must be able to devise ways to help develop the small neighborhoods they dwell in to erode some of the resistance and indifference there, something present in almost every society toward incoming foreigners.

At the risk of sounding repetitive, it is essentially imperative that black Americans who are genuinely seeking to live in Africa and reintegrate into the African societies endeavor to respect the humanity of the Africans and not look down upon them as inferior beings or view them and their actions and ways of living with skepticism, unconscious suspicion, and rude questioning by denigrating their mannerisms and traditions, like equating eating with their hands with primitive and barbaric behavior, as many do.

If the black Americans go to Africa with such superior know-it-all attitudes, the natives will in time dance for them because of the high value of their dollars but ultimately will not dance with them, which is crucial for their societal integration.

Also it crucial for Africans and black Americans living in the same neighborhoods to form block associations or neighborhood groups to meet periodically to discuss important issues affecting their blocks, and this will make the new black Americans become involved and immersed in their new society, and they will begin to understand the nuances or the dynamics operating in their new society.

The worst thing that the black Americans can do in any African society is isolate themselves and live like bunch of foreigners or arrogant Americans. Then they will deny themselves the opportunity to become part and parcel of their new society.

It is vital for the incoming black Americans to join as many local groups, clubs, and associations, and attempt to assimilate into the new African society by understanding some of the local languages for their own protection.

Perhaps black Americans, because they have no tribal affiliations, will be the force to break down the lingering tribal animosities that have created so much political and civil unrest in African nations.

It therefore behooves African politicians and statesmen to seriously work to integrate interested black Americans into their societal fabric and genuinely embrace them as their long-lost brothers and sisters, like Joseph embraced his brothers in Egypt.

CONCLUSION

WE THANK THE MANY BLACK Americans and Africans who willingly or angrily, in some cases, participated in this quest to understand our people a little better, and we have noted all they advised and said about each other. For our part though, we have come to see the similarities between both the Africans and the black Americans. It must be noted that both the black American and the African were enslaved by people of European descent.

The African slavery was given fanciful word *colonialism*, which simply means the capture of our people for economic and social exploitation. Similarly, black Americans were also captured, colonized, and enslaved. But behind all these fanciful words, the condition of both our people on each side of the Atlantic Ocean amounted to some of the following:

- Both people were Africans separated from each other and living in various parts of the world under European domination and exploitation.
- Both Africans did not have the freedom to do as they please, but had to obey and follow the dictates of European powers.
- The worldview of both the black American and the African were conditioned by their European masters
- Our conversion to Christianity and Christian values, beliefs, and morals was inculcated into us by these same European colonialists and exploiters who enslaved us.
- The educational system that thoroughly brainwashed our people to look up to the European as a superman and to view the African as an inferior species had similar origins.
- Both the African and black American attained "independence" from Europeans. Black Americans' emancipation from chattel slavery was called the abolition of slavery, and their subsequent "right" to vote and participate in their society took place during the riots of the 1960s, the so-called civil rights movements. In Africa, the nationalist patriotic movements led to the political decolonization of the continent, which is fashionably referred to as "independence" from the same European powers.
- After these great movements in the 1960s for both our people, we both were living under the economic, political, and social superstructure controlled by these same European powers. Though our condition has somewhat changed, we are still essentially under European domination.

- The cardinal difference was that the African was fighting for the independence of his country, while the black American was fighting to get a piece of the American pie that his ancestors had worked hard to bake.

Again, a theme throughout our conversations with many of our African respondents is that black Americans continue to look down upon the Africans.

Many still cling to the archaic and obsolete perceptions of the age-old and worn-out Tarzan, wrinkled Jane, and puking cheetah, even in this new millennium. Africans are understandably upset about their brothers and sisters still looking condescendingly at them.

Some Africans are fearful that someday black Americans—in their hostility, rage, and retribution seeking—will capture Africa and create a similar governmental structure the freed slaves established in Liberia.

Most of us recall that the freed slaves in Liberia, the so-called Americo-Liberians, created a tyrannical apartheid-like government and excluded the native Liberians by controlling all stages of the governmental structure while systematically oppressing the so-called inferior native Liberians.

We consider this view as alarmist, and what happened in Liberia cannot happen on the African continent again, because of the increased political and economic development and the wholesale advancement in education of many Africans, especially those who have studied in the various America universities and those who have simply lived and worked abroad.

Also it is instructive to note that perhaps the emerging political paradigm of globalization will be inconsistent with political colonialism of new territories, bearing in mind that we are painfully aware of the newly emerging neo-colonialism around the world today.

We are very much aware of the changing trends, particularly during this era of globalization. We are aware that many black Americans surf the Internet and not only educate themselves on the Worldwide Web, but visit the various African websites to learn more about Africa.

Additionally, large numbers of black Americans are visiting Africa, and some are opting to stay for longer periods of time, while others are raising their families there.

Our co-author, Roxanna, belongs to the African American Association of Ghana (AAAG). This powerful association of African Americans is instrumental in helping Ghanaians in various philanthropic and humanitarian ways that we are so grateful to mention here. We are also aware that there are other philanthropic black American associations all over the African continent, America, Canada, Europe, and the West Indies.

We commend such great enterprises that seek the upliftment of our people. Additionally there are countless anonymous individuals who are spending all kinds of funds, trying desperately to elevate the Africans on the continent.

We have to mention the visionary work of Reverend Leon H. Sullivan, the powerful organizer of Africa-African American Summits. Some of the achievements of this great patriot are summarized below:

> We have spent a great deal of effort on debt relief. I made trips to several European countries and talked with President Clinton to get as much debt relief for Africa as possible. I received commitment of the Paris Club to put debt relief for Africa on the main agenda of the next Group of Seven meeting in Naples, Italy. Follow –up debt relief initiatives resulted in more than $2 billion in debt relief for sub-Saharan Africa.

Sullivan added: The first African-American Summit resulted in a US Congressional hearing on issues that affect sub-Saharan Africa and a special United Nations session on debt relief for Africa. Other major initiatives include Teachers for Africa Programme, a Best and Brightest African Bankers Training programme that will train hundreds of African bankers to help with the development of their banking systems..

We are developing medical projects for the containment of AIDS and the eradication of river blindness, particularly in Nigeria; we are launching Schools for Africa Programme, and for the next 10 years I would like to see a thousand schools built in rural areas where they don't exist. I work half of my time following up on what happened at that Summit. At the next summit, I expect at least 500 African businesses and 300 African-American businesses. I expect at thousands of 'average' African-Americans to attend. 11

Similarly, the coordinator of the Constituency for Africa, Melvin P. Foote, encouraged Africans to "reciprocate African-American gestures by forming business associations with African American businesses, 'instead of dealing with white businesses alone, they [Africans] have got to look to African-Americans who have the same expertise.

We should reach out to each other just like the Jews, the Poles, and the Irish reach out to each other. I think right now we are in the woods. But if we work, together, we will get out of the woods. We've got to get out of the woods." 12

It is also instructive to point out that many black Americans are slowly discovering their roots, especially after epic *Roots* miniseries aired in national theatres and on television networks all around the globe. We are proud to note that there are many black Americans giving their children African names; we encourage them to continue with this proud heritage. They should also understand that all African names have meanings.

For example, among the Akans of Ghana, the first names of children are named after the days of the week:

- A boy born on Monday is named **Kwadwo or Kojo,** and a girl born on the same day is called **Adwoa or Adjoa.**
- A boy born on Tuesday is **Kwabena or Cobbinah**, and a girl is **Abenaa.**
- A boy born on Wednesday is **Kwaku or Kweku,** and a girl is **Akua or Ekua.**
- A boy born on Thursday is **Yaw,** and a girl is **Yaa.**
- A boy born on Friday is **Kofi,** and a girl is **Afua or Effua.**
- A boy born on Saturday is **Kwame,** and a girl is **Amma.**
- A boy born on Sunday is **Kwasi** or **Kwesi,** and a girl is **Akosua.**

We also took the liberty of asking many black American men why they put rings in their noses and earrings in their ears—sometimes in both ears. Interestingly, a lot of the black men told us that they are identifying with their African brothers and sisters.

We reminded them that African men do not put rings in their noses and most seriously frown upon seeing real black men putting earrings in their ears like women. Such practices are not part of the African tradition per se, but they date back to the unfortunate era of slavery.

A ring in the nose during these unfortunate times identified a particular tribe of slaves.

Kwame's ninety-year-old uncle, Abusua-Panyin Kwame Sikayena, informed us that the fashionable earrings in males' ears are a throwback to the slave eras, when one earring in a man's ear denoted a slave of certain origin and those with two earrings were of another ancestral origin.

He told Kwame that once the elders of the society saw the men with the earrings, they immediately knew them as slaves from a specific ancestry. He told us that some of the earrings were bigger, which meant the slave was very valuable, while those with little earrings had little material value.

We strongly challenge male youngsters who are blindly putting earrings on to study the origins of this tradition and desist such useless fashions because there is nothing African about them.

We strongly encourage them to identify with Africa all the time and to first study and understand what they are identifying with as positive Africanism. We discourage them from practices that Africans are distancing themselves from.

We would also like to mention that we have met several black Americans who have converted to become priests and priestess of the great Akonnedi shrine in Larteh in Ghana. Our coauthor Kwame has taught several of them the Twi language at the African poetry theatre in Jamaica, Queens in New York.

We concur with many respondents who challenged the Africans on the continent to move heaven and earth to modernize their nations. Such modernization involves the practice of good governance, which will mean the establishment of political stability, which would guarantee and protect individual freedoms and insure the rule of law.

We strongly believe that with the creation and maintenance of political stability in Africa, many black American entrepreneurs, with ingenuity and professionalism, would be willing to set up all kinds of businesses in Africa to provide employment and increased revenue, which would improve the standard of living of the populations on the continent.

It is also an observable fact that the Chinese people were accorded their respect all over the world after Chairman Mao led the Cultural Revolution, which made China a great nation. Similarly, the Japanese gained their respect after they consolidated and built their huge economy after their defeat in World War II.

Here we would like to take the liberty to challenge Africans on the continent. The time has come. The winds of change are blowing nearer and nearer. The heavens and the gods are throwing the Africans a challenge. The Almighty God himself is beckoning the African to wake up from his deep slumber and unify at least the West African periphery into the new West African States. We strongly believe that with the creation and political cementation of the West African States, a new market and subsequent development would catapult the entire region into a politically powerful entity that would transform the negative image of black people worldwide.

Perhaps, with this new positive black image, our people from both sides of the Atlantic would remove and bury the chains of mental slavery that have for centuries prevented us from openly championing our own African personality.

We conclude by echoing that no matter how we feel and think about each other, black Americans and Africans are inseperable, because we are indelibly linked together, and in the powerful words of Reverned Martin Luther King Jr. ... "We are tied together in a garment of mutuality. What happens in Johannesburg affects Birmingham, however indirectly. We are descendants of the Africans. Our heritage is Africa. We should never seek to break the ties, nor should the Africans." 13

NOTES

1. Charles A. Reich, *The Greening of America* (New York, NY: Bantam Books, 1971) p. 15

2. Hal Urban, *Positive Words, Powerful Results* (New York, NY: Simon & Schuster, 2004) p. 38

3. Sherry Anderson and Patricia Hopkins, *The Feminine Face of God: The Unfolding of the Sacred in Women* (New York, NY: Bantam Books, 1991) p. 7

4. *The Willie Lynch Letter and The Making of a Slave* (Chicago IL: Lushena Books, 1999) pp. 7-9

5. We asked black Americans to answer these questions:
    *   Can you give us your first name?
    *   What state and city were you born in?
    *   Do you refer to yourself as African American and why?
    *   Do you refer to yourself as a black American and why?
    *   Where were you raised?
    *   What is your educational background?
    *   What is your professional background?
    *   Are you single, married, or widowed?

- When you hear "Africa" what comes to your mind?
- Why do you think the way you do about Africa?
- How did you come by this information?
- How did you first hear or learn about Africa?
- Today, what do you know about Africa?
- How did you come by this information?
- Name five countries in Africa.
- Name five cities in Africa.
- Name five presidents in Africa.
- Name five rivers in Africa.
- Have you ever been to Africa, and where did you visit?
- Did you meet Tarzan and Jane? How old were they?
- Would you consider living in Africa, and why or why not?
- Have you ever met an African, and where?
- What were your first impressions of him or her?
- Have you ever dated an African?
- Would you consider dating one and why?
- Have you had any type of relationship with an African?
- What was the nature of the relationship?
- Would you consider marrying an African and why?
- Have you ever worked with an African, and in what capacity?
- What were your impressions of him?
- Did you attend any schooling with an African?
- What was your experience with the African schoolmate?
- In your estimation, do you believe the African thinks he or she is better than the average black American?
- Give reasons for your answer.
- Do you respect the African as an equal human being and why?
- Do you think the African is a little inferior to you and why?
- Do you know any African history?
- What do you know about African history?
- How can the black Americans and Africans come together?

6. We also asked African people the following questions:
- What is your name?
- What African country were you born and raised in?
- What did you know about black Americans before coming to America?
- How did you get this information about the black Americans?
- How long have you been in America?
- Where in America did you attend school?
- What do you do currently in America?
- Are you married?
- Do you have any relationship with a black American?
- Do you have any black American friends?
- How do they treat you (and be specific)?
- Do you believe the black American thinks he or she is superior to you and why?
- What is the meaning of the word *akata* to you?
- Why do Africans call black Americans akata?
- Now that you have lived in America for some time, do you still think of the black Americans as you did before and why?
- Have you worked with black Americans before?
- What were your impressions of working with them?
- Have you ever dated a black American?
- How did your partner treat you generally?
- Would you consider marrying a black American?
- In your estimation, the black American's condition in USA can be attributed to what?
- Why do you suppose there are many black boys in jails today in America?
- Why do you think drugs are a pervasive problem in the black community today?
- Why do you think there is a higher incidence of teenage pregnancy among black Americans?
- In your estimation, why is the divorce rate high among black Americans?
- How can the black family structure be strengthened?

- How can the black Americans and Africans come together?

7. Valerie Melissa Babb, "To Ghana and Back," Africana Heritage;
Vol. 6, No. 3, 2006, pg. 11. A publication of the Schomburg Center for Black Culture. The New York Public Library; 515 Malcolm X Boulevard, New York, NY 10037

8. Kwame Nkrumah, *Dark Days in Ghana* (London: Panaf Books Ltd.1967) p.49

9. Ronald Kessler, *Inside the CIA, Revealing the Secrets of the World's Most Powerful Spy Agency* (New York: Pocket Books, 1992) p. 3

10 Valerie Melissa Babb, p.5

11 West Africa Number 3986 February 21-27 1994 p.302

12 West Africa No.3986 p.302

13 West Africa No.3986 p.298

SPECIAL THANKS

THE AUTHORS WISH TO EXPRESS their sincere thanks to Ms. Tina Ashley of Randolph Center for her many suggestions, valuable insight, and help during the preparation of this manuscript.

We also want to extend our thanks to Justice Abeyie for his help, the many examples he provided for us, and his vital insight into black Americans and African relationships.

To Shad Ansah and Kwame A. Insaidoo Jr, your lively and heated discussions around the kitchen table helped us to understand how the modern youngsters feel about this explosive topic. And to Robert A. Insaidoo, we thank you for allowing us to use parts of your upcoming book to explain ourselves better in our work.

We also would like to thank the many participants in Africa, especially Alahassan Mohammad Hardi of the University of Ghana, for passing out our questionnaires to the students and sending us their responses. And we also thank our numerous respondents in American and those from the Caribbean Islands who willingly participated in answering our often intrusive questions.

ABOUT THE AUTHORS

KWAME A. INSAIDOO:

Kwame A. Insaidoo was born in Ghana, West Africa. He received his early education from Akwasiho Presbyterian Middle School, Fijai Secondary School, and Aggrey Memorial Zion secondary school. While at the University of Ghana, he was awarded an academic scholarship to attend Southwest Missouri State University, where he was elected president of Association of International Students. Kwame is also a member of Missouri chapter of Omicron Delta Epsilon Economic Honor Society. In 1979 he graduated with a bachelor's degree in economics.

Kwame attended graduate school at New York University, where he received his master's degree in 1988. He is also the author of *Can the Black Man Rule Himself,*? And *Is the Bible a Woman's Enemy?*.

Kwame and his wife, coauthor Roxanna, and their two children. Kwame Jr. and Robert work and reside in New York City.

ROXANNA PEARSON INSAIDOO

Roxanna Pearson Insaidoo was born in Buffalo, New York. She attended Helene Fuld College of Nursing and graduated in 1991. Ms Pearson was elected vice president of her graduating class and successfully passed her New York State board examination. She has been working as a registered nurse in hospitals and public health services specializing in psychiatric and geriatric nursing care.